FAREWELL

TO THE CHIEF

FAREWELL
TO THE CHIEF

Former Presidents
in American Public Life

EDITED BY RICHARD NORTON SMITH

AND TIMOTHY WALCH

Foreword by Don W. Wilson
Archivist of the United States

Afterword by Gerald R. Ford
38th President of the United States

HIGH PLAINS
PUBLISHING CO., INC.
Worland, Wyoming

Library of Congress Catalog Card Number: 90-91626

ISBN 0-9623333-2-8 (Cloth)
ISBN 0-962333-3-6 (Paper)

Designed by Cameron Poulter

Photos courtesy of presidential libraries

High Plains Publishing Company, Inc.
P. O. Box 1860
Worland, Wyoming 82401

Contents

Foreword

DON W. WILSON

In the autumn of 1932, former President Calvin Coolidge filled out a membership form from the Washington Press Club. At the place marked "Occupation," he wrote in "retired." Then he skipped down a line to the section marked "Comments." Coolidge thought for a moment before writing: "And glad of it."

George Washington might have said very nearly the same thing, albeit in slightly less taciturn language. Yet "Farmer" Washington was nearly called from retirement in 1798 to fight a war with revolutionary France. Thomas Jefferson left the White House to found a great university. John Quincy Adams swallowed his pride and became a congressman; his subsequent fight against slavery and for the right of petition earned him the title "Old Man Eloquent." Martin Van Buren ran for the presidency as a Free Soil candidate; Millard Fillmore sought electoral vindication in 1856 as nominee of the Know Nothings. For whatever it's worth, he carried only one state—Maryland.

Seven years after Andrew Johnson survived an impeachment attempt, the former president came back to haunt the Senate that had nearly convicted him of high crimes and misdemeanors. Ulysses Grant toured the world, waging a long-distance campaign that won him more votes in Tokyo than Toledo. William Howard Taft found belated happiness as chief justice of the United States. Woodrow Wilson refused to run for the Senate because, as he put it, "The Senate isn't worth a damn . . . Besides, I'd just get in a row with old Lodge." And the aforementioned Mr. Coolidge wore a more dour than usual expression following the collapse of Wall Street and the onset of hard times in 1929.

What all these men had in common was their uncommon membership in a very select fraternity—what Herbert Hoover whimsically labeled "my exclusive trade union." Until Harry Truman joined up in 1953, Hoover was alone in the club of living former presidents. Today, by contrast, his trade union is prospering with four members in good standing.

Based on a conference held in October 1989 at the Hoover Presidential Library, this collection of essays is among the first efforts to discuss the role and responsibilities of America's former presidents. The essays trace the evolution of a singular office through the lives of eleven men who occupied the presidency and went on to new useful roles as public servants without portfolio. Some of these men have sought to regain their old address on Pennsylvania Avenue. Others have been content to serve as advisers at large on things in general.

There is no set pattern to the ex-presidency, for each president is different. So is each presidential library. I say this from a position of some authority. Before becoming Archivist of the United States, I served as director of the Ford Library and Museum and, before that, as assistant director at the Dwight D. Eisenhower Library and Museum in Abilene, Kansas. So you will forgive me if I admit up front to a little bias on the subject of the American presidency and the libraries that interpret the office and the men who have held the office to millions of citizens. Presidential libraries are not designed to be personal monuments. Rather, they are historical treasure troves and classrooms of democracy. In recent years, especially, they have become popular places for Americans of all ages to examine a past not always learned in school.

One reason for their popularity is each library's growing presentation of public programs. Attendance at the Hoover Presidential Library, for example, more than doubled between 1987 and 1989. Visitors come to see exhibits of national importance and to take part in events ranging from a bicentennial reenactment of George Washington's first inaugural address to a World War I preparedness parade that coincided with the museum's retrospective on "the Great War." The success of the Hoover Library is in direct proportion to its appeal to the vast number of Americans who are interested in their country's heritage, who are curious about their political ancestry, and who are seeking connections in an age when so much of our society seems fragmented.

One final point. I have long believed that the National Archives can and ought to become a cultural resource of national significance. This volume—and the conference that generated it—suggests one of the most vital ways in which the Archives can take history out of a vault in Washington, D.C., and share it with those to whom it naturally belongs. At the risk of offending my fellow academics, I am bold enough to say that history is too important to leave to the historians. Thanks to this collection of essays—jointly sponsored by two of the nation's eight presidential libraries—we can learn as much about America as its highest office. We can also learn a good deal about ourselves. For whatever Mr. Coolidge might have written in 1932, there is one thing we can never retire, and that is our curiosity.

Introduction

Not long after his defeat in the 1912 presidential election, William Howard Taft delivered a wry valedictory before New York's Lotos Club. His theme: What are we to do with our former presidents? With his tongue firmly in cheek, Taft proposed "a dose of chloroform or . . . the fruit of the lotos tree" as a means to protect his countrymen "from the troublesome fear that the occupant [of the nation's highest office] could ever come back." What is more, he said, such decisive methods would relieve the former president himself "from the burden of thinking how he is to support himself and his family, fix his place in history, and enable the public to pass on to new men and new measures." As for William Jennings Bryan's suggestion that all former presidents become ex-officio members of the Senate, Taft was dubious. "If I must go and disappear into oblivion," he chuckled, "I prefer to go by the chloroform or lotos method. It's pleasanter and less drawn out."

Jests aside, Taft asked an important question. Almost eighty years later, we Americans have yet to define a role for our former presidents. In recent years, former presidents have drawn fire from a number of congressmen and other critics who fear that the "imperial presidency" is turning into a similarly extravagant retirement, complete with Secret Service protection for widows and children, "fat" book deals, handsome offices, and bloated staffs as well as presidential libraries that more nearly resemble monuments than research institutions.

Certainly today's former presidents seem to have little in common with John Adams who farmed at Quincy, James Monroe who lived with his daughter in New York because debts forced him to sell his Virginia estate, Franklin Pierce who braved the pro-Union taunts of his New Hampshire neighbors, Theodore Roosevelt on African safari, or Calvin Coolidge who retired to a $32-a-month duplex in Northampton, Massachusetts.

And what about Taft? He taught law at Yale before serving as chairman of Woodrow Wilson's War Labor Board and finally attaining the goal of a lifetime in 1921 when Warren Harding named him chief justice of the United States. Near the end of his long and productive life, Taft observed with evident pleasure: "I have forgotten that I ever was President."

It was an observation Herbert Hoover might sometimes have wished that he could have made during his thirty-one years out of office. Indeed, the fact that Mr. Hoover served the longest ex-presidency in American history made the Hoover Presidential Library and Museum a logical setting for a conference on this perplexing question of what to do with our former presidents. Thus the Hoover Library and the Gerald R. Ford Presidential Library and Museum jointly assembled an impressive roster of historians, journalists, former presidential staff members, and one member of what Hoover himself called "my exclusive trade union" to examine the history of the post-presidential years of Theodore Roosevelt to Jimmy Carter and beyond.

This volume offers readers the substance of that two-day conference. The essays that follow will be of interest to the casual student of American history as well as to scholars of the presidency. They represent an important step toward a fuller understanding of the ex-presidency, its evolution, rewards, and perils.

The book is divided into chapters that focus on both past and present aspects of this singular office. In the first four chapters, eight distinguished historians and biographers analyze the post–White House years of presidents from Theodore Roosevelt to Dwight Eisenhower. In Chapters 5 and 6, personal aides and advisers to Presidents Lyndon Johnson, Richard Nixon, and Jimmy Carter offer their recollections of working with these uniquely powerful leaders in their twilight years. Chapter 7 focuses on the role former presidents should take in the future. Former Librarian of Congress Daniel J. Boorstin, President Gerald R. Ford, and journalists Roger Mudd and Helen Thomas, among others, discuss Dr. Boorstin's provocative suggestion to establish a new national council, a House of Experience, to institutionalize the ex-presidency and disseminate the ideas and insights of former presidents through the national media. The volume concludes with President Ford's Afterword—his personal reflections on the role of former presidents in American public life.

Several dozen people must be acknowledged for their substantive contributions to the success of the conference and this volume. Foremost, we want to express our continuing gratitude to President Ford and his fellow contributors for their participation in this timely conference. It is their hard work that made the gathering a success and this volume worthy of publication.

We also want to acknowledge the support of Archivist of the United States Don W. Wilson and Assistant Archivist for Presidential Libraries John T. Fawcett. Their aid and encouragement were important in the early stages of conference planning; both men also were active participants in the proceedings.

The advice and counsel of Frank Mackaman, director of the Gerald R. Ford Library and Museum, was vital. In truth, the conference would not have been possible without the co-sponsorship of the Gerald R. Ford Library and Museum. Throughout, Frank was the epitome of scholarly cooperation and assistance.

We also want to recognize the contributions of our colleagues who served as session chairmen during the conference: Steven A. Kesselman of the Herbert Hoover National Historic Site, Ellis W. Hawley of the University of Iowa, Bennedict K. Zobrist of the Harry S. Truman Library, John E. Wickman of the Dwight D. Eisenhower Library, and F. Forbes Olberg of the Hoover Presidential Library Association.

Many groups worked behind the scenes to make the conference run smoothly. Special recognition must go to National Park Service staff members for their extensive support in providing parking, traffic, and crowd control during President Ford's visit. We are also grateful to Iowa Public Television for providing camera coverage of the key conference sessions, to West Music of Iowa City for providing audio assistance, to Hartwig Motors of Iowa City for transport shuttle services, and to the Ambassadors of the Iowa City Chamber of Commerce for their many helping hands.

We were particularly proud of the contributions made by the docents of the Hoover Library, who greatly eased the logistical burden of planning and conducting a conference of this magnitude. Recognition goes to Lori Detweiler, Joan Hemingway, Eleanor Luckel, Kathleen McLaughlin, Gertrude MacQueen, Bill Oglesby, Del Orr, Ed Spencer, and Michael Triplett for their fine work.

Above all, however, the conference succeeded due to tireless efforts by the combined staffs of the Hoover Presidential Library Association and the Hoover Presidential Library and

Museum. Their willingness to work long, hard, and harmoniously was as commendable as it was predictable. Special plaudits go to Tom Walsh, executive director of the Library Association, who handled conference publicity and ran the press room; and to Judy Kaesar, the adminstrative officer of the association, who took on the time-consuming task of conference registration. The continued support of the association makes possible many vital library and museum activities.

Not enough can be said about the Hoover Library staff, the General Services Administration custodians, and the Hoover Library guard force. Each of these groups exhibited new talents and resiliency; each took on difficult assignments with enthusiasm. Would that we had the space to list all that they did during those two days. A list of their names will have to suffice: Don Barnhart, Jim Barnhart, Joan Cahill, Chris Christensen, Floyd Christensen, Jim Detlefsen, Janlyn Ewald, Jim Fulwider, Leon Gebert, Maureen Harding, Pam Hinkhouse, Rosemary Hora, Ervin Larson, Barbara McGuire, Joan Maske, Mildred Mather, Dale Mayer, Dwight Miller, Paul Mohr, Richard Myrvik, Cora Pedersen, Jennifer Pedersen, Kim Porter, David Quinlan, Richard Rex, Kim Marie Smith, Shirley Sondergard, Patrick Wildenberg, and Cindy Worrell.

We know that all of the individuals who contributed to the conference join us in hoping that this small volume will stimulate more serious discussion of an important issue and generate an increased public awareness of the role of former presidents in American public life. Perhaps the pages that follow can serve as something of a civics lesson, bringing readers in closer contact with the ideas of historians, journalists, political scientists, government officials, and a former president. At its core, however, we hope that this volume, like the conference it commemorates, will encourage public appreciation of history as a pathway of understanding between what has been and what becomes as a result of it.

Richard Norton Smith
Timothy Walch
West Branch, Iowa
Presidents Day, 1990

President Woodrow Wilson with Former President William H. Taft.

I

FOUR STUDIES
IN FRUSTRATION:
FROM TR
TO COOLIDGE

For all their disappointments and frustrations as former presidents, Roosevelt and Wilson might have savored the underlying similarity in their roles. Both were statesmen whose greatness went beyond big deeds done while wielding power. Their greatness lay even more in the ways that they drew upon the past for ideas and inspiration to inform the present and mold the future in pursuit of public good. Their ex-presidencies were a piece with the deeper meaning of their careers. Nothing so became each man in his presidency as the leaving of it.

Using their own resources and talents, William Howard Taft and Calvin Coolidge made the most of their time as "that melancholy product of the American governmental system. . . ." For Taft these years were a bridge to the job he most wanted: chief justice. For Coolidge, it marked a dignified retirement. . . . In his remark that "it is difficult for me to go anywhere. They will not leave me alone," there is caught some of the opportunities and burdens that all former presidents confront and that current research is designed to illuminate.

—John Milton Cooper, Jr.

—Lewis L. Gould

Lonesome Lion and Crippled Prophet: Theodore Roosevelt and Woodrow Wilson as Former Presidents

JOHN MILTON COOPER, JR.

Nearly everything about Theodore Roosevelt and Woodrow Wilson as former presidents seems to throw them into contrast. In March 1909 Roosevelt had just turned fifty years old. He was the youngest person to step down from the presidential office before or since. Twelve years later, in March 1921, Wilson was sixty-four years old. He was the oldest man to go out of office in sixty years and the third oldest former president in almost a century.

More than age separated the two men when they left the White House. Roosevelt departed from the presidential mansion full of his familiar vigor and strength. He spent his first post-presidential year on a prolonged hunting and naturalist's safari in Africa, followed by a triumphal public tour of western Europe. Wilson moved only a mile away from his former domicile, and he was both physically and emotionally impaired by the effects of severe cerebrovascular strokes. Although he made a formal stab at practicing law in Washington, Wilson actually lived in retirement and seldom ventured outside his house on S Street except to be taken for rides in his automobile.

Similarly, these two men's ex-presidencies varied in length and public impact. Roosevelt's life and career after leaving the White House lasted just two months short of ten years, until his death in January 1919. During that time, he remained a major force in American politics, and at least twice in those years he exerted a larger influence on the nation's public affairs than anyone else, even his two presidential successors. Wilson's ex-presidency lasted less than a third as long: He died in February 1924, not quite three years after leaving office. During that brief span, he remained a shadowy figure in public life, as he issued occasional statements to the press, published only one short magazine article, and spoke a few words in public on rare occasions, including one brief statement over the new medium of radio. In all, Wilson played little direct role in public affairs during his final years.

Yet did these men's ex-presidencies really offer such a stark contrast as outward circumstances seem to indicate? If they did, that in itself would be a remarkable contrast. It would fly in the face of the deep affinities and strong similarities that linked their presidencies and the bulk of their active careers in and out of politics. For all the apparent contrasts between the two men—"Teddy" versus Woodrow, the Warrior versus the Priest—Roosevelt and Wilson shared a common identity as political intellectuals. They both believed that ideas must inform and refine the exercise of power and that ideas must fulfill those functions not just as matters of technical expertise or strategic plans but fundamentally as philosophical guides. In these convictions, Theodore Roosevelt and Woodrow Wilson stood as historical throwbacks to the founding days of the American republic. Their true presidential peers were John Adams, Thomas Jefferson, James Madison, and John Quincy Adams. In common with those men, Roosevelt and Wilson possessed a dimension of intellectual sophistication and depth that they shared with none of their other predecessors and none of their successors.

Moreover, although fundamental differences in philosophy did divide them, the two men took similar stands on the major issues of domestic and foreign policy of their time far more often than they opposed each other. The question remains, therefore: Did Roosevelt and Wilson really differ so greatly as former presidents?

In one respect, the answer must be an emphatic yes. Theodore Roosevelt still stands as the most active of all former presidents. No one has ever matched him in physical and mental vigor, whether it was on the African hunting trail, in the jungles of South America, on the campaign hustings, or at his desk writing books, magazine articles and editorials, and newspaper columns.

No one has ever matched him in public influence, either. He was not the only former president to run again. Martin Van Buren and Millard Fillmore had preceded him as third-party candidates after leaving the White House, while Grover Cleveland had previously regained a major party nomination and won another term. But Roosevelt's running again in 1912, first for the Republican nomination and then at the head of the Progressive party ticket, almost certainly altered the course of American political history, not least by insuring the election of his greatest rival, Woodrow Wilson. Again, four years later, when Roosevelt ruthlessly smothered his new party in order to mount a united front against Wilson's reelection, he contributed more than anyone else to Republican nominee Charles Evans Hughes's nearest of misses in 1916. Finally, in the last year of his life, Roosevelt started to make the greatest political comeback of any former president, and he was the odds-on favorite for the Republican nomination and likely election in 1920.

Woodrow Wilson, by contrast, stands as the least active of all former presidents. The reason is simple. To this day, Wilson has been the only person to leave the presidential office incapacitated. James K. Polk and Chester A. Arthur both lived shorter times after stepping down, and Andrew

5

Jackson suffered from a host of infirmities in his last years. But no other former chief executive has labored under the burdens of partial paralysis, limited vision, shortened attention span, and feeble emotional control that plagued Wilson after the strokes that he had suffered in 1919. His disabilities prevented him from visiting his law office more than twice for brief periods, from reading any length of time, and from writing anything more than his signature. The only public appearances that Wilson made as former president occurred when he hobbled out on his doorstep on the anniversaries of the armistice that ended World War I and, ironically, to ride in the funeral procession of his apparently healthy presidential successor, Warren G. Harding. Otherwise, Wilson participated in public life as former president solely through his single short radio address and magazine article, through advice to friends and supporters who visited or corresponded with him, and through occasional statements to the press. His health prevented him from taking part in the 1922 congressional contests, the only elections that occurred during his lifetime after he left the White House.

Still, despite those indisputable contrasts, the question of whether Roosevelt and Wilson differed so much as former presidents has not been exhausted. In another respect, the answer to that question must be an emphatic no. The dissimilarity in the two men's circumstances did not prevent them from making an essentially similar political contribution as former presidents. Both of them set the major ideological agendas for their parties and for the mainstream of national politics.

Theodore Roosevelt's activity during his first five years after leaving office shaped the positions of the two major parties and his new third party on domestic issues involving regulation of business and extension of democratic participation in politics and government. In one way, Wilson, through his New Freedom programs, reaped where Roosevelt had sown. In another way, Roosevelt laid the basis for the reunification of the Republican party and its hegemony in the 1920s. During the second half of his ex-presidential decade, Roosevelt played as great a part as anyone in awakening Americans to involvement in international affairs, and his became one of the most influential voices to the great debate that began then over the role of the United States in world politics. It is fascinating but ultimately fanciful to speculate about the impact that Roosevelt might have had at home and abroad if he had lived another few years into the 1920s.

Woodrow Wilson's ex-presidency really began before his term expired. It began when he suffered his disabling stroke in October 1919, and it continued during the next four or five months, as public knowledge spread that he would never recover sufficiently to function fully as president. Yet despite his incapacity, Wilson was easily the dominant presence at his party's 1920 convention. His aegis even helped to launch another political career when thirty-eight-year-old Franklin D. Roosevelt conspicuously paraded the New York state banner in the unplanned, emotional demonstration that greeted the unveiling of Wilson's portrait at that convention. Such visibility, together with the younger Roosevelt's politically potent surname, helped him gain the Democratic party's vice-presidential nomination in 1920, and although his ticket lost badly, national exposure later boosted his gubernatorial and presidential nominations. Also, during the 1920 campaign, Franklin Roosevelt and James M. Cox, the party's presidential nominees, were so moved by their meeting at the White House with Wilson that they spontaneously pledged to make the president's overriding foreign policy goal—membership in the League of Nations—their own major issue.

Nor, in a sense, did Wilson's ex-presidency end with his

death early in 1924. In 1924 and 1928, Democratic platforms once more committed the party to the extension of Wilson's New Freedom programs at home and to membership in the League of Nations. Later Franklin Roosevelt's New Deal displaced the New Freedom as the Democrats' domestic policy lodestone, but Wilson's earlier initiatives and directions had clearly laid much of the basis for the New Deal. However, during the upsurge of isolationist sentiment in the 1930s, Franklin Roosevelt himself repudiated League membership in his quest for the 1932 presidential nomination and Wilson's reputation suffered severe devaluation. Starting at the end of that decade, however, and escalating during World War II, Wilson's stature as a leader in international affairs rose to new heights of apotheosis. Books, magazines, and even the movies leaped aboard the Wilson bandwagon as his historical reputation underwent the most spectacular resurrection of any American president. Only the death of Franklin Roosevelt in 1945 and the impact of his memory really closed Wilson's posthumous ex-presidency.

In the final analysis, Theodore Roosevelt and Woodrow Wilson did play fundamentally similar roles as former presidents. One was the lonesome lion, prematurely and by his own unwise choice exiled from the leadership of his pride. Roosevelt spent a decade in the political wilderness, but even without official power he exerted enormous influence. At the end, the old lion was about to take his place again at the head of the pride. The other was the prophet crippled by the infirmities of his physical constitution. Wilson spent the last five years of his life as a voice crying in the wilderness, but even without seeing his goals attained he made himself heard not only in the few years that remained to him but much more significantly during the two decades after his death. Within a generation, the prophet's visions at home and abroad had become the foundation of national policy for the rest of the century.

For all their disappointments and frustrations as former presidents, Roosevelt and Wilson might have savored the underlying similarity in their roles. Both were statesmen whose greatness went beyond big deeds done while wielding power. Their greatness lay even more in the ways that they drew upon the past for ideas and inspiration to inform the present and mold the future in pursuit of public good. Their ex-presidencies were of a piece with the deeper meaning of their careers. Nothing so became each man in his presidency as the leaving of it.

"Big Bill" and "Silent Cal:"
William Howard Taft and Calvin Coolidge
as Former Presidents

LEWIS L. GOULD

On February 24, 1914, Calvin Coolidge, then a member of the Massachusetts Senate, wrote to William Howard Taft to compliment the former president on articles he had recently written for the *Saturday Evening Post.* "I cannot help feeling," Coolidge wrote, "that you may be performing a public service greater and more important than what you could have done had you still been president." When Coolidge commented about Taft's post-presidential activities, he had no idea that he would one day share the status of former president. In fact for a year in 1929-1930 the two men would be co-members of what Taft in the November 1916 issue of *Current Opinion* had called "the ex-Presidents Club," an organization that, as Taft put it, "has not a large membership."

William Howard Taft spent seventeen years as a former president, the last nine of which were as chief justice of the United States. To compare the post-presidencies of Taft and Coolidge, his post-presidential years extended from March each was a private citizen. In the case of Taft, that period was from March 4, 1913, when Woodrow Wilson succeeded him, to June 30, 1921, when the Senate confirmed Warren G. Harding's nomination of Taft as chief justice. For Calvin Coolidge, their post-presidential years extended from March 4, 1929, when "the little man," as Hiram Johnson called him, left Washington for Massachusetts until his death on January 5, 1933.

What do the retirement years of Taft and Coolidge disclose about that interesting phenomenon of the post-presidency? They indicate something about the diverse ways in which the American people have regarded the president and his office during the early years of this century. For both Taft and Coolidge, the years after the presidency were not as institutionalized or formalized as they have become in modern times. These men had no pensions, no cadre of Secret Service men to guard them, no presidential libraries, and no named foundations. "It's a trying, even an unhappy role— that of maintaining the dignity of a President of the United States, minus the authority, minus the salary," wrote Congressman J. Hampton Moore in his 1925 book *Roosevelt and the Old Guard*. Taft and Coolidge were former presidents in what might be called the premodern era of that status. After leaving the White House, they had to build lives based on their own reputation and resources.

Their situation reflected changes that had occurred in public expectations about the president in and out of office. The nineteenth-century view had been that the chief executive was only the "first citizen" of the nation. Just as a sitting president should not campaign for reelection, a former president should return to his people for a dignified repose with no pension, no trappings of office, and no rewards from his term except the satisfaction of a duty performed. As Lord Bryce wrote in his classic study *The American Commonwealth*, a former president "soon sinks into the crowd or avoids neglect by retirement."

By the early years of this century, however, the status of ex-presidents changed. Theodore Roosevelt had a high degree of responsibility for this development. His fame and charisma riveted attention on the White House, while his flamboyant ex-presidency kept him in the national spotlight. But there were also forces at work that went beyond the magnetic Roosevelt to make former presidents more than passive elder statesmen.

As a result of the emergence of a mass media and the mechanisms of celebrity, the president of the United States had become famous and familiar to his fellow citizens. Out of office, he found that newspapers and journals wanted comments on news events, audiences gathered to hear his reflections, and reporters covered his activities. Former presidents found that they were marketable assets. In the case of both Taft and Coolidge, the post-presidency was a time of balancing a desire for quiet in retirement with a need to accommodate and to some extent exploit the continuing popular curiosity about their character and personalities.

William Howard Taft spent a very active eight years between 1913 and 1921. He was Kent Professor of Law at Yale College and also a professor of constitutional law at Yale Law School. He pursued a vigorous round of lecturing, writing for periodicals, and public service. During World War I, he was joint chairman of the National War Labor Board. One of his most ardent interests was the League to Enforce Peace and the battle to establish a League of Nations following World War I.

Throughout this period Taft displayed an acute awareness of his status as a former president. He refrained from attacking Woodrow Wilson publicly because "the minister who is removed from the pulpit and put in a pew never thinks much of the sermons of his successor." During the period of American neutrality between 1914 and 1917, Taft avoided the kind of harsh criticism that Theodore Roosevelt poured on Wilson. "We must abide by the judgment of those to whom we have intrusted the authority," Taft said in February 1915, "and when the President shall act, we must stand by him to the end." Privately, as a dedicated Republican, Taft was more critical. Wilson was, he wrote to his wife in October

1916, "perfectly ruthless and unscrupulous, but many people regard him as a saint."

A more pressing personal need for Taft as a former president was a dependable income. He told E. F. Bennett in December 1913: "They don't pension ex-presidents, and the wolf is not quite so far from the door of 367 Prospect Street, New Haven, as it was from the White House." His salary at Yale was $5,000 a year to start, reaching $6,000 a year by 1918. That was a substantial reduction from the $75,000 that the president earned, plus the $25,000 for expenses. The salary was, however, a comfortable one, the largest that Yale paid to a member of its faculty.

To supplement his salary, Taft crisscrossed the nation speaking to a variety of organizations such as the National Geographic Society, the Union League Club of Philadelphia, and the Electrical Manufacturers Club on diverse issues such as judicial recall and the duties of citizenship. His secretary, Warren Mischler, arranged for the "honoraria" that usually averaged about $400 per appearance. As Mischler recalled, "I could book him as far as Iowa, to lecture there on a Saturday night, for then he could take the midnight train out of there on a Saturday night, and get back to New Haven in ample time for his first lecture on Monday." The round of lectures and appearances agreed with the former president. "I frisk about the country a good deal," he wrote to Oliver Wendell Holmes in December 1913, "but the freedom from the great official responsibility is a greater relief than I realized when I was in office."

A trademark of William Howard Taft was his size. He was probably the fattest president in American history, weighing more than 340 pounds at the end of his term. The most famous story about his size was the telegram he sent to Elihu Root, then secretary of war, from the Philippines. After a mountain journey, Taft wired Root: "Stood trip well. Rode

horseback twenty-five miles to five thousand feet elevation."
Root immediately replied: "Referring to your telegram . . .
how is the horse?" When Taft came to Yale, he went on a
diet that the dean of Yale Medical School had specified. By
late 1913 his weight had fallen to 270 pounds. News stories
mentioned his weight loss, and Taft was besieged with requests from advice-seekers about how to reduce. In letters
and interviews, he shared his method with the curious public
who had sent him fan mail. "I have dropped potatoes from
my bill of fare," he said, "and also bread in all forms. Pork
is taboo, as well as other meats in which there is a large
percentage of fat." To exercise, Taft also played golf as often
as possible. After losing a match in 1913, he expressed his
rage in the clubhouse. A colleague observed: "Why, you feel
worse about being beaten at golf than you did on losing the
presidency!" Taft replied: "Well, I do, *now!*"

Another source of income for Taft was writing, and he
published prolifically during these years. His articles appeared in the *Saturday Evening Post* ("Votes for Women"),
in the *Independent* ("Arbitration Treaties that Mean Something"), and in the *Ladies Home Journal* ("The College Slouch,"
in which the former president complained of "the indifferent
manners and slouchy dress among the students" at the nation's colleges). In these writings Taft articulated his conservative political and social views in a manner that many
Americans found attractive. "If all ex-Presidents were like
Mr. Taft," wrote the editors of *The Nation* in January 1915,
"the old question what shall we do with them would soon
cease to be asked."

One subject that Taft spoke and wrote on readily was the
presidency itself. In an article for the *Saturday Evening Post*
in February 1914, he revealed that if he had achieved a
second term, he had planned to travel to the Philippines to
break with the tradition of a president not leaving the United

States during his term of office. He noted, however, that he would have first asked Congress to approve his plans with a resolution and would have gone if it had refused their permission. Taft delivered several series of lectures titled "Our Chief Magistrate and His Powers," which were later published. To his audiences, he said, "I claim no special learning from books as to the presidency, but I can bring practical experience that the necessary paucity in living ex-Presidents makes somewhat exceptional." In his remarks he only touched on the differences between his own view of presidential power and the more expansive interpretation that Theodore Roosevelt advanced between 1904 and 1913. Noting that Roosevelt had divided all presidents into two groups and designated them as "Lincoln Presidents" and "Buchanan Presidents," he then wryly observed that "in order more fully to illustrate his division of Presidents on their merits, he places himself in the Lincoln class of Presidents and me in the Buchanan class." While his lectures read somewhat dryly today, they offer an interesting conservative analysis of the office. His judgment that Roosevelt's stewardship theory of the office, which attributed "an undefined residuum of power to the President," was "an unsafe doctrine" that "might lead under emergencies to results of an arbitrary character doing irremediable justice to private right" has more resonance now than it did in 1915.

Taft recognized that his 1912 defeat ended his career as an electoral politician. In mid-1914, however, his political allies discussed the possibility that he might be a candidate for a congressional seat in the Connecticut district of which New Haven was a part. Their aim was to see him run again for the presidency. Taft thought of the post as a platform from which he might address judicial reform through membership on the House Judiciary Committee. Though he had been critical of the idea proposed by William Jennings Bryan (in his Lotos Club speech of 1912) to give former presidents a nonvoting seat in the Senate, Taft gave the idea of a House race serious thought before he decided during the summer of 1914 that he should not do it. He concluded that his candidacy would be seen as a political comeback bid and his real motives would be misunderstood.

Taft left no comment on the initiative made by Congressman J. Hampton Moore in late 1916 to sponsor legislation to create a permanent House seat for former presidents at a salary of $25,000 a year. Instead, Taft went on with his good works as a retired chief executive. He contributed his time and name to the Red Cross during World War I, fought hard for the League of Nations through his membership in the League to Enforce Peace, and added his support to the fortunes of Republican candidates down through the election of 1920. His party's success in that contest brought the election of Warren G. Harding and in due course Taft's nomination for chief justice during the summer of 1921. When his name came before the Senate in executive session, there were only four negative votes. Hiram Johnson opposed him because of old political battles and also because, as he told his sons in July 1921, Taft had chosen "to become a cheap talker for cheap fees at Chautauqua, and a petty scribbler for small remuneration, rather than practice his profession when he had the opportunity, of living his life in the dignity befitting an ex-President." Johnson's verdict had more bile than balance. Taft had, on the whole, met well the public demands on ex-presidents to be useful citizens while not becoming a partisan scold of his successor. The years between the presidency and the Supreme Court were an interesting period in Taft's life, and one that merits more attention than it has so far received.

One of the few serious studies of the phenomenon of the post-presidency argued that "Calvin Coolidge's insignificant

Vermont retirement has little interest." Since the former president divided his residence between Northampton, Massachusetts, and Plymouth, Vermont, the judgment is not geographically accurate. More important, Coolidge was more active and in the public eye than this comment indicates. His post-presidential phase, though only about four years long, reveals the extent to which fame and celebrity had become inescapable aspects of the lives of former chief executives.

In his autobiography that was published in 1929, Coolidge observed: "We draw our Presidents from the people. It is a wholesome thing for them to return to the people. I came from them. I wish to be one of them again." He regarded it as fortunate that presidents "are not supported at public expense after leaving office, so that they are not expected to set an example encouraging to a leisure class." In fact, he concluded, "it is becoming for them to engage in some dignified employment where they can be of service as others are."

Returning to the people had its ambivalent aspects as the Coolidges soon discovered when they began living in the small duplex at 21 Massasoit Street in Northampton. Public interest in their lives continued after March 1929. Tourists came to town to get a glimpse of the presidential couple. A neighbor wrote in 1930 that "hundreds of automobiles from every state pass the house every day," sometimes as often as one every six seconds. The onlookers stopped, often took pictures, and on occasion posed "on the steps or in front of the house where some members of the party" took pictures "to show their friends at home." Sometimes they even asked the former president and his wife to pose with them.

The duplex was clearly inadequate, and the Coolidges moved in 1930 to a more spacious and less accessible residence, The Beeches, which cost them $40,000 for its twelve rooms and nine acres. The newspapers reported that they had sixteen rooms, but Mrs. Coolidge commented: "There are four rooms we can't find." A visiting friend said to her: "It surely agrees with you to be home," and the former First Lady replied: "You just can't imagine how good it is."

They appreciated their home even more once they had tried to indulge their desire to travel. They went first to Florida without incident, and then Coolidge wrote ahead to New Orleans, asking the postmaster of that city to get them rooms without telling the newspapers. The inevitable took place, and a crowd of five thousand people met the Coolidges at the station. Similar scenes occurred during the rest of their journey. After that, the ex-president limited his excursions to necessary monthly visits to New York for his duties on the board of the New York Life Insurance Company and for journeys in the New England area. As he wrote to his former secretary Edward Clark in March 1932: "I have kept away from Washington because I get so much newspaper reaction if I go anywhere that the only place I am safe is at home. All the newspapers expect me to function just the same as if I were in public office." He wryly observed to Bruce Barton, who had come to see him, that "people seem to think the presidential machinery should be kept running even after the power has turned off."

Writing offered Coolidge the chance at "some dignified employment" without the need to deal with public clamor. His first product was the series of reminiscent articles that became *The Autobiography of Calvin Coolidge*. That terse work sold very well and suggested that a continuing market existed for the president's prose. He wrote other essays ("What It Means to be President," "The President Lives Under A Multitude of Eyes") for such journals as the *Saturday Evening Post, Cosmopolitan*, and *Ladies Home Journal*.

Coolidge also wrote a daily newspaper column that appeared nationally for a year under the titles "Thinking Things Over With Calvin Coolidge" or "Calvin Coolidge Says." He wrote these columns in pencil, carefully counting the number of words that he used. He earned several hundred thousand dollars for this assignment, which one wag dubbed "Syndicatin' Calvin and his straight face stuff." However, a great deal of public attention followed what he said. His remarks tended toward the vague and general. "The people at large have a great interest in economy in public expenditure," was one insight, as was "Everyone knows that the government is not perfect." These words lent themselves to parody, and a liberal journal produced some under the title "Cluckings of Calvin." Another critic said that "what Mr. Coolidge is selling is not himself, but the factitious glitter of the presidency."

As the political fortunes of Herbert Hoover and the Republicans worsened after 1929, many in the GOP looked back fondly to Coolidge, his tranquil presidency, and his continuing fame. Exhausted from his time in office and suffering from severe allergies and asthma, the former president had few illusions about a political comeback. "A retired President ought to be an example of loyal support to his successor," he wrote in late 1931 in what the press took to be an endorsement of Hoover. For the most part, Coolidge resisted efforts to be drawn back into politics. "I cannot conceive any circumstances that would persuade me to make a speech," he said in late October 1930 during the Massachusetts campaign.

He did yield to Republican importunities two years later and made an address at Madison Square Garden on Hoover's behalf. The speech was not a success, in part because of the condition of the president's allergic throat. But it reflected his distance from the center of national politics. "After being out of things for three years it is about the same as though you had never been in it so far as any knowledge of what is going on and the issues at stake," he noted in September 1932. By December he said, "I feel worn out," and he responded to those who wanted him to think of the presidency once more: "I could not pick it up again. I imagine that was one trouble Cleveland had in trying to administer a second term. Any time you hear anybody talking of me, just tell them to stop it." Within a week Coolidge was dead.

By the early 1930s it was evident that former presidents could no longer even pretend to slip back into the obscure private life that Lord Bryce had discussed and which Hiram Johnson had favored. Both Taft and Coolidge found that their notoriety was an asset that could help overcome the absence of a pension for an ex-president. The experience that Coolidge and his wife faced in their travels also foreshadowed the need that some modern presidents would feel for Secret Service protection or some sort of entourage when they met the public. There was as yet no focused analysis on the situation of the former chief executives and no real proposals to use them effectively or to provide them with the means to build a new career. Using their own resources and talents, William Howard Taft and Calvin Coolidge had made the most of their time as "that melancholy product of the American governmental system," as Winthrop Sheldon put it in his book *Ex-Presidents of the United States.*

For Taft these years were a bridge to the job he most wanted: chief justice. For Coolidge, it marked a dignified retirement during which he once lamented: "It's my past life that makes all the trouble—if I could only get rid of my past life! But that always stays with one." He concluded, "It is difficult for me to go anywhere. They will not leave me alone." Coolidge's words caught some of the opportunities and the burdens that all former presidents confront and that recent research has illuminated.

Former President Herbert Hoover dedicating a new Boys' Club.

II

AN UNCOMMON
FORMER PRESIDENT

In his books and speeches, his commissions, foreign travels, and above all in his relief efforts, Hoover crafted an ex-presidency richer in accomplishment and more poignant emotionally than any before or since. In the end, he gained something much finer than vindication; he became an extraordinarily useful citizen, in the words of an admiring editor, "counselor to the republic." It is a role coveted by each of his successors.

From Hoover's kaleidoscopic ex-presidency, then, we may adduce this model of a modern former president. He should live a long life; be blessed with excellent health and superabundant energy; have a source of income that frees him for public service; have a far-flung legion of friends willing to labor on his behalf; feel a passionate need to justify his record before his countrymen and posterity; have a philosophy of life that imbues in him a consuming desire to achieve, to build great institutions that will survive him, and to serve his fellow men and women unstintingly. And one thing more: He should possess an utter unwillingness to fade away.

—Richard Norton Smith

—George H. Nash

Outliving the Bastards:
Herbert Hoover
as a Former President

RICHARD NORTON SMITH

Not long before he died, Herbert Hoover was asked how he had managed to survive the wilderness years that began in 1933 and ended only with the death of his onetime friend and later antagonist, Franklin D. Roosevelt. His reply was typically pungent: "I outlived the bastards." More reflectively, he liked to say that if you waited long enough, the wheel would turn, the pendulum swing. It was a bittersweet assessment, one that dramatically underplayed Hoover's own struggle to regain at least a measure of the prestige he had once enjoyed as "the Great Humanitarian."

Few in the spring of 1933 would have forecast such a comeback. Some of Hoover's friends looked at the exhausted president, 25 pounds thinner than when he took office, whose face had become a base-relief of the nation's suffering, and questioned whether he could survive twelve months. On March 4, with the nation's banks tottering, Herbert Hoover climbed into a car for the mirthless ride down Pennsylvania Avenue and excommunication to the warm, spicy countryside around Palo Alto. He departed Washington without a job, his life in politics apparently at an end, his future in doubt, and his record in the hands of his enemies.

Fate had cast him as black bishop to Roosevelt's white knight. Everywhere, Americans that year were singing "Who's Afraid of the Big Bad Wolf"; psychologists attributed the song's popularity to public relief at the exit of the man

Father Charles Coughlin dubbed "the Holy Ghost of the rich, the protective angel of Wall Street." A St. Louis movie-house patron struck his neighbor, an absolute stranger—and told the police he was justified because the man resembled Hoover. There were rumors that the former president was bound for Europe on Andrew Mellon's yacht or that he was absconding with the gold of Fort Knox.

Hoover himself believed that he was under surveillance, at one point mischievously adding a postscript to a letter that had been opened, asking its reader to please save him the trouble of forwarding it directly to the Roosevelt White House. In the spring of 1934, the hotel room of Hoover's private secretary was broken into during the same week IRS agents showed up to conduct an audit of the former president's tax returns.

These were the years of gall and wormwood, when friends could find Hoover in his Palo Alto study, playing solitaire and railing against his successor for sleights real or imagined. FDR went off the gold standard that spring and Hoover made no public protest. Even recognition of the Soviet Union in November 1933 found him keeping his own counsel— although it did spark work on the vast and yet unpublished magnum opus he called "Freedom Betrayed," three profusely documented volumes on U.S. foreign policy that he would work on for the next thirty years.

Perhaps more than any other former president, Hoover sought vindication as a writer. If he could no longer shape history, he would at least have the satisfaction of interpreting it. His first literary undertaking after leaving the White House was a deliberately impersonal volume. Yet *The Challenge to Liberty* was also Hoover's reentry into the political arena, a polemical shot across Roosevelt's bow. Its author was careful to disassociate himself from Al Smith and other critics in the business world who had formed the Liberty League to rant against Rooseveltian treachery.

As Hoover put it, "I am no more fond of the Wall Street model of liberty, than I am of the Pennsylvania Avenue model." All the same, he was alarmed enough to assail debased currency, limits on production, and a government competing with private enterprise. What Hoover termed "the tragedy of Liberty" followed a similar pattern on both sides of the Atlantic: "idealism without realism, slogans, phrases and statements destructive to confidence in existing institutions, demands for violent action against slowly curable ills; unfair representation that sporadic wickedness is the system itself." Next came the man on horseback, demanding delegation of authority from elected representatives, denouncing all opposition and exploiting propagandists in the pay of the state. Wrote Hoover, "Liberty dies of the water from her own well—free speech—poisoned by untruth."

Critics responded by painting the former president as a man with a theory. Having raised him to the presidency, it shackled his imagination and paved the way for his ultimate defeat. According to this school of thought, Hoover was a victim of his own certainties. Not the least of his problems lay within his own party. For millions of rank and file Republicans, Hoover was the New Deal's most credible foe. To GOP leaders he was a tar baby par excellence, "Daddy Warbucks" with a Havana cigar clenched between his teeth. For fifty years Democrats would reap a rich harvest of voter resentment just by mentioning his name. It is hard to know for whom this was more painful—Hoover himself or Republican candidates starting with Alf Landon in 1936.

Through it all, Hoover campaigned as he wrote, out of a genuine anxiety for the future of liberty—and of the classical liberalism that produced both freedom and abundance. The structure of human betterment, he said, "cannot be built upon foundations of materialism or business, but upon the bedrock of individual character in free men and women. It must be built by those who, holding to ideals of high purpose, using the molds of justice, lay brick upon brick from the materials of scientific research, the painstaking sifting of truth from collections of fact and experience, the advancing ideas, morals and spiritual inspirations. Any other foundations are sand, any other mold is distorted; and any other bricks are without straw." These words were spoken by the man who had once declared, "The only trouble with capitalism is capitalists—they're too damned greedy!"

The Challenge to Liberty set the tone for years of barnstorming against the New Deal. FDR skewered his critics by telling of a nice old gentleman who fell off the dock in 1933 and was rescued, only to complain three years later that he had lost his hat. Hoover responded that "the old gentleman was surreptitiously pushed off the dock in order that the hero could gain the plaudits of the crowd as a life saver."

Writing in the wake of Landon's crushing defeat, Hoover sounded a note of despair. "The economic situation is bad," he claimed. "The total failure of the Roosevelt Administration to grasp the fundamentals of what is needed is worse; and the disintegration of the Republican Party due to the efforts of a dozen pinheads does not offer much hope for real leadership." He was not always so outspoken. Prior to going abroad in 1938, Hoover was asked about the delicacy of his diplomatic position. No doubt he would be required to raise his glass to the health of the president of the United States. He might even be asked to compliment Roosevelt's foreign policy. That was no problem, said Hoover—he could keep quiet in seven different languages.

His subsequent encounter with Hitler was both dramatic and banal. The German dictator seemed perfectly rational until mention of two subjects—democracy and the Jews—sent him into one of his patented tirades. Hoover would later confide to friends that Hitler seemed "a little insane."

His own efforts to avert U.S. involvement in the war, coupled with a barely concealed campaign for his party's 1940 nomination, led to fresh controversy. Whatever one thinks of Hoover's attitudes toward England and Germany, one cannot read his writings of the period without being deeply moved. Repeatedly, he said that he did not care what people's politics were: so long as their bellies were empty, he wanted them filled. In World War I, such beliefs had prompted Winston Churchill to call him a son of a bitch. In World War II, they would prevent Hoover, his Committee to Aid the Small Democracies, and his Commission for the Relief of Poland from providing more than a trickle of relief supplies early in the fighting.

Even more than his Quaker upbringing, Hoover's memories of World War I had disabused him of any notion that war is some kind of glorious pageant. Instead, he recalled the filth, the stench, and the automated death of the western front. He penned a haunting memoir of the Battle of the Somme and a muddy battlefield contested by vast stationary armies.

"Here and there," he wrote, "like ants, they advanced under the thunder and belching volcanoes of 10,000 guns. Their lives were thrown away until half a million died. Passing close by were unending lines of men plodding along the right side of the road to the front, not with drums and bands, but with saddened resignation. Down the left side came the unending lines of wounded men, staggering among stretchers and ambulances. Do you think one can forget that?" he asked plaintively. "And it was but one battle of a hundred!"

When war came, he argued vigorously that Hitler and Stalin should be allowed to tear each other apart, like two

Kilkenny cats quarreling over Europe. "I am afraid that we are lepers in a country which has gone over to the unspeakable intolerance of war psychosis," he lamented, before adding with more than a touch of self-righteousness that "truth has never been timed to suit the tastes of people who do not want to hear it. In view of the way the Preacher was treated, it would seem that the Sermon on the Mount was badly timed."

After Pearl Harbor, Bernard Baruch was called to the White House, ostensibly to consult with the president on homefront organization. Baruch began by saying that if he were undertaking any large-scale operation, the first man he would turn to was Herbert Hoover. What's more, he continued, he happened to know that Hoover was available. Roosevelt looked his friend straight in the eye. "Well," he snapped, "I'm not Jesus Christ, and I'm not raising him from the dead."

Hoover never stopped protesting the inconsistency of aiding a Soviet dictator under the guise of preserving freedom. When his own party embraced various postwar schemes full of eloquent rhetoric, Hoover beseeched it to avoid repeating the tragic nobility of Versailles. Together with Hugh Gibson, he dashed off another volume, *The Problems of Lasting Peace*, this time urging Americans to put aside revenge as the guiding motive of peacetime settlement. In his blueprint for the postwar world, Hoover wanted emotions to cool before institutions were formed. He wanted less reparations, more chance for genuine economic recovery.

With this in mind, he went to see Harry Truman in the first days of the new administration, armed with a plan Henry Stimson called "rather radical." It urged the new president to go on the radio and tell the people of Japan that they could keep their Emperor—not to mention Korea and Formosa. In return, they must give back Manchuria, throw in their hand, and lay down their weapons. This would keep the Russian bear out of the Far East, Hoover reasoned, forestalling a repeat of Stalin's European annexations.

Truman rejected the advice, only to seek Hoover's involvement on another front—that of postwar relief. In 1946, at the age of seventy-two, Hoover made a voyage of reconciliation to thirty-eight nations. He accepted a $5,000 offer from *Look* magazine to describe his travels, on condition the money be sent to the Boys' School of Bagdad. Elsewhere, Hoover renewed his acquaintance with Pope Pius XII, dismissed Mahatma Gandhi as a soapbox politician, and in Buenos Aires stoically announced his willingness to eat dirt if that was what it would take to get his hands on Argentine foodstuffs.

Early in 1947 the former president undertook a survey of the shattered German Reich, which he called his "positively last job." Before it was over, he had taught the Germans to eat cornmeal and located enough warehoused food to provide 3.5 million school-aged youngsters with one hot meal a day. It was immediately dubbed the "Hoover *Speisung.*" When CARE was created in the fall of 1945 using Army surplus rations, it was under the guidance of General William Haskell, who twenty years earlier had aided the "Great Engineer" in meeting the desperate needs of postwar Russia.

In a radio address to the American people, Hoover described 800 million homes without food. "Hunger is a silent visitor who comes like a shadow," he said. "He sits beside every anxious mother three times each day. . . . All the values of right living melt before his invasions, and every advance of civilization crumbles. But we can save these people from the worst, if we will." And then, as if for emphasis, he added, "We do not want the American flag flying over nation-wide Buchenwalds."

Hoover returned home to a new assignment from the Truman White House, a massive reorganization of a federal establishment bloated by war. For the next two years, the former president and his colleagues, in what came to be known as the Hoover Commission, pored over the ramparts of an entrenched bureaucracy. Hoover personally authored each of the commission's sixteen reports, at 9,000 words designed to be carried on a single page of the *New York Times*. In one of them he quoted approvingly from Hamilton's *Federalist Paper No. 70* on behalf of a strong executive. He argued the case for a cabinet secretariat, even an administrative vice president assigned to oversee the budget.

While the first Hoover Commission saved a few billion dollars, its most lasting and ironic impact may have been on conservative Republicans at last reconciled to an expansive presidency. The second Hoover Commission, convened in 1953, proposed still more sweeping changes. In the end, fewer than one-third of its recommendations were enacted. Hoover did get his way when Congress authorized a new Department of Health, Education and Welfare. And as late as 1961, Robert McNamara was using Hoover's reports to reform Pentagon administration and procurement.

In their autumn years Hoover and Truman became America's most enduring "Odd Couple." They waged a tongue-in-cheek debate over whether to admit Dwight Eisenhower to their exclusive trade union. The temperature in Independence, Missouri, was 91° on the summer day in 1957 when Hoover helped his friend open a presidential library. Afterward, a fluttery admirer approached the two men to ask exactly what former presidents did with their days. "Madame," Hoover informed her, "we spend our time taking pills and dedicating libraries."

His own schedule suggested otherwise. There was money to be raised for Stanford University—and campus architecture to be opposed as a modern affront to the Romanesque bell tower of the Hoover Institution. There were his beloved "pavement boys" for whom Hoover would raise more than $100 million during thirty years as president of the Boys' Clubs of America. There were honorary degrees to add to the eighty or so already accumulated, an endless avalanche of mail to occupy his five secretaries, and book after book.

At the Waldorf Towers, where he shunned the party-going ethic of neighbors like Elsa Maxwell and the Duke and Duchess of Windsor, Hoover worked on four volumes, simultaneously. Long after FDR's death, a house guest was astounded to discover the old man sitting behind his desk, before dawn, scribbling away. "I'm making my Roosevelt book more pungent," he said—and no further explanation was called for. *The Ordeal of Woodrow Wilson* was a surprise bestseller, a sympathetic account of the wartime president undone by his own idealism in the diplomatic snakepit.

In his eighty-fifth year, Hoover traveled 14,000 miles, delivered 20 speeches, accepted 23 awards, and answered 21,000 letters. He also wondered why his Waldorf neighbor Douglas MacArthur was so inactive. After all, reasoned Hoover, the general was a younger man, born in 1880 instead of 1874. Following John Kennedy's narrow victory over Richard Nixon, Hoover brought the two men together for a postelection meeting in Florida. He turned down, on the grounds of age, the president-elect's invitation to serve as honorary chairman of the Peace Corps. But he corresponded with George McGovern, the youthful director of Food for Peace, and he refused to bar grain shipments to Communist China.

Late in 1962, his health gave way, and Herbert Hoover, Jr., put the Kennedy White House on notice to prepare for a state funeral. The next morning, the boy called "Bub" was astonished to find the old man sitting up in bed calling for his pipe. "We're back in business," said Hoover. And so he was.

By then, Hoover could joke that he was the only person of distinction in all history to have a worldwide depression named after him. More seriously, he confessed, "My education was that of an engineer. I do not know all the nuances of economics." It was at times like this, in what he liked to call his "years of acknowledgment," that Hoover spoke poignantly of his boyhood and of the sudden awareness that did not come until he was twelve years old that he could do a thing simply for the pleasure it gave, without engendering the Lord's wrath.

There were two things no man should be forced to do in public, Hoover often said. One was pray; the other was fish. So he wrote a book on fishing, extolling its democratic joys, "for all men are equal before fish." He also published a charming book of letters to and from children.

Hoover mailed out Christmas greetings with denunciations of Godless communism and mourned the fact that doctors denied him at age eighty-nine *both* Beluga caviar and his rightful share of what he called "old character builder." Yet he welcomed his induction into the Bohemian Grove's Old Guard. "There is something to be said for all the Old Guards in the world," Hoover declared. "They are men past the time when they want anything on this earth but the welfare of those who they guard. Their tempers have been softened in the solution of experience. They have learned that virtue is a more stable currency than the commodity dollar. They are a menace to the fuzzy-minded, the foolish, and all New Deals."

Shattered by news of John Kennedy's murder, the next morning Hoover passed word to the Johnson White House that he was anxious to be of service to his country in any capacity, "from office boy up." As the years passed, a gentle decrescendo began in Waldorf Suite 31A. Outside, Americans too young to have felt the sting of 1933 came to regard

Hoover as a kind of crusty Dutch uncle.

Not long before his death, Hoover impulsively asked a young friend what she wanted out of life. The woman thought this over, then replied, truthfully enough, that her life was nearly perfect. She loved her husband, her family, her home. For her, the status quo was enough. Herbert Hoover drew back in horror. "How can you say such a thing," he asked, making no attempt to conceal his disapproval. "I want more. I want more friends. I want to write better books. I just want more."

Hoover never stopped wanting more. In that, he was a faithful reflection of his countrymen. He has often been hailed or jeered as the founder of rugged individualism. In truth, he was in the tradition of other Americans, including our greatest native thinker, who pronounced his own unshakable belief in national progress through individual advance. America, wrote Emerson in days of heady optimism, was "the Country of the future . . . a country of beginnings, of projects, of designs, of expectations."

At his best, Herbert Hoover embodied Emerson's country of the future. When he died, his life had covered nearly half its history and shaped some of its most tumultuous decades. Walter Lippmann was not alone in suggesting that Hoover ought to be remembered as a humanitarian instead of a politician, a man run over by historical forces and condemned to spend his days resisting the trends of his times.

But there was more to it than that. In his books and speeches, his commissions, foreign travels, and above all in his relief efforts, Hoover crafted an ex-presidency richer in accomplishment and more poignant emotionally than any before or since. In the end, he gained something much finer than vindication; he became an extraordinarily useful citizen, in the words of an admiring editor, "counselor to the republic." It is a role coveted by each of his successors.

Achieving Post-Presidential Greatness:
Lessons from Herbert Hoover

GEORGE H. NASH

On a cool October morning in 1964, Herbert Hoover died in New York City at the age of ninety years, two months, and ten days. His life had spanned nearly half the length of the American republic. At the time of his passing, he had spent more than fifty years—half a century—in public service. It was a record that in sheer scope and duration may be without parallel in our history.

If Herbert Hoover was the paradigmatic modern former president, it is appropriate to ask: What are the crucial components of the paradigm? At least as much as Theodore Roosevelt, Hoover came to personify the activist ex-presidency. What, then, were the essential ingredients of his success?

We must first acknowledge that in one respect Hoover's ex-presidency has not been emulated by his successors. For two decades after 1932, during the bitter Republican exile from the White House, and in some ways until his death, Hoover remained a partisan—a tireless and very public castigator of the dominant political currents of his day. Now all modern former presidents engage to some degree in what I would call ritualistic political activity, such as addressing their party's nominating conventions, campaigning for like-minded candidates, and working the so-called mashed potato circuit. But for Hoover this activity was never ritualistic. He behaved as a committed ideological warrior more persistently and more fervently than any of the former presidents who followed him.

Why? Partly, I believe, because of what he himself once called his "naturally combative disposition," partly because of the searing circumstances of his repudiation at the polls and shabby treatment by the man who defeated him, but most of all because he perceived the New Deal of Franklin Roosevelt to be a revolutionary transformation in America's political economy and constitutional order. And having seen the unpalatable future, he could not bring himself to acquiesce. For him, unlike his successors, the New Deal did not seem irreversible. He therefore could not content himself with avuncular, above-the-fray, elder statesmanship—the kind of pattern toward which the ex-presidency is now evolving. More than his successors to date, he chose to be both partisan and nonpartisan simultaneously.

In other respects, however, the Hooverian ex-presidency continues to seem archetypical. What were the factors that made it so, the factors that underlay his comeback?

Let us begin with the basics. The first requirement for post-presidential success is longevity, and here Hoover was supremely successful. In 1933 he left the White House a comparatively young man, a man in fact still in his fifties. He lived on as a former president for thirty-one and one-half years—longer in that role than any other occupant of our highest office. During these decades he not only outlived most of his political enemies but also witnessed an abatement of the storms of the 1930s. He further benefited from the human tendency to confer honorific status on any public figure who attains an advanced age. By the time elder statesmen turn eighty, he once remarked wryly, they are politically "harmless."

A second trait that made Hoover's productive "twilight" years possible was his remarkably robust constitution. For nearly all his life the engineer-turned-statesman was blessed with exceptionally good health and a phenomenal capacity for work. And when in later years an occasional illness did strike, he refused to let it encumber him. Hence, in 1947, he launched the first Hoover Commission while suffering a tormenting case of shingles. Similarly, in 1958, less than three months after a gall bladder operation that some did not expect him to survive, he flew to Belgium as President Dwight Eisenhower's personal envoy to the Brussels World Fair. Even in his mid-eighties he worked eight to twelve hours a day. Between the ages of eighty-five and ninety, he published a four-volume history of his gigantic relief efforts in World Wars I and II; he called it *An American Epic*. Sinclair Lewis once observed that the secret of success is to "make the seat of your pants adhere to the seat of your chair for long enough." This was one of Hoover's secrets also.

But there was more to his physical make-up than simple good health and stamina. Hoover was endowed with an extraordinary amount of nervous energy. One of his closest friends, Will Irwin, asserted in 1916 that Hoover did not need to exercise to control his weight. At times, Irwin wrote, Hoover "fairly thinks himself thin." A man who worked with him at the United States Food Administration in 1917 claimed that Hoover's pulse always exceeded 100 beats a minute—and sometimes went up to 125. I am not certain that this observer was correct, but Hoover did have a number of habits—such as jingling the change in his pocket—that revealed an inwardly nervous disposition. Only while fishing did he appear fully to relax, but one suspects that even then his thoughts were often elsewhere.

Hoover, in fact, was incapable of extended repose. "His mind was never still," one of his grandchildren once said. Often, in his later years at his apartment in New York City, he would awaken at two o'clock in the morning and go to work. On these occasions he would open a can of soup, heat it, gulp it down, and then proceed to write until four in the morning.

A third key to Hoover's productivity was his financial security. Living largely before the days of the subsidized ex-presidency, he possessed a comfortable income derived ultimately from his pre-1914 success as a mining engineer and investor. While not especially imposing by today's standards, his savings nevertheless enabled him to devote himself unceasingly to public service. They also permitted him to maximize his influence in a variety of ways. Maintaining a residence at the Waldorf-Astoria, for instance, along with a staff of secretaries and research assistants, must have cost him thousands—eventually tens of thousands—of dollars a year. But Hoover very deliberately assumed this expense as the price of being where he wanted to be: at the epicenter of American political and intellectual life. Similarly, in 1934, when his manifesto *The Challenge to Liberty* was published, he and associates distributed the book assiduously. Nearly 11,000 copies were sent to libraries throughout the United States and another 2,500 to newspaper editorialists. Hoover personally gave 13,000 copies to prominent people. In all likelihood the cost of this immense effort was borne, directly or indirectly, by Hoover himself. It was a practice that he repeated with every book that he subsequently published—a deliberate form of influence-building that only a man of some means could afford.

Hoover's customary writing procedure in his later years provides a further illustration of this point. First, he would compose his book manuscript in longhand. Then his draft would be typed, revised by Hoover, and set in printer's galleys so that he could acquire a sense of how the book would look in print. Then he would *revise the galleys*— repeatedly—until as many as ten or even more successive sets of galleys or page proofs had been prepared. Such a process must have been enormously expensive, but, again, Hoover possessed the resources to be a perfectionist.

A fourth reason that the defeated president was able to recover from the obloquy of 1932 lay in his astonishing array of friendships. From his earliest days as a mine manager, he displayed an uncanny ability to select men of talent and turn them into loyalists for life. Why was he able to engender such boundless devotion? One source of his appeal was his personal example of self-sacrifice and total dedication. Another was a management style that encouraged subordinates to take the initiative and do all they could for their leader. Still another source of bonding—and a potent one indeed—was the altruistic character of the humanitarian relief efforts that made him famous. It has been said that Herbert Hoover was responsible for saving more lives than any other person in history. For many who worked with him in these missions, the experience was the most exhilarating one of their lives. Some, like Robert Taft and Lewis Strauss, held him in almost filial esteem.

An unbreakable cord of idealism drew these and other Hooverites to the man they revered as "the Chief." They provided him an independent political base in the 1920s. They constituted a personal following and nationwide intelligence network after 1933. In nearly every major city in America there were "Hoover men" eager to distribute his books, arrange for local radio stations to carry his nationally broadcast speeches, defend him in letters to the press, and otherwise rally to his side. I can think of no other former president, with the exception, perhaps, of Theodore Roosevelt, of whom the same could be said. Like the hero of San Juan Hill, Hoover in his years of "retirement" commanded a following based in part upon his *non*political, *pre*political achievements. It helped to insure his presence in what he once called the "big game" of public life.

Yet longevity, good health, driving energy, wealth, and admiring friends do not alone explain the Hoover phenomenon. In a sense these were only preconditions for his success: necessary but not sufficient. Three additional factors—*volitional* factors—gave his ex-presidency its singular intensity and productivity. First, more than any other chief executive in our history, Hoover, after he left the White House, felt impelled to defend his previous conduct as a public servant. The quest for vindication was perhaps the dominant theme of his later life. It found expression in his crusade against the New Deal, his campaign for presidential renomination in 1940, his attempt to have himself appointed senator from California when Hiram Johnson died in 1945, his assistance to scholars engaged in revisionist history, and, above all, his unending series of books: three volumes of memoirs (only a fraction of what he actually wrote), four volumes of *An American Epic*, eight volumes of post-presidential addresses, a partly autobiographical work entitled *The Ordeal of Woodrow Wilson*, and a huge, multivolume, never-published indictment of Franklin Roosevelt's foreign policy.

If all this seems quixotic, remember: Hoover left office during our greatest national trauma since the Civil War. He was vilified and hated as no other American in his lifetime. Remember, too, that *before* his presidency his career trajectory had curved unbrokenly upward. Until the Great Depression he had never truly experienced defeat. These circumstances, combined with his own unique temperament, forged in him an unbending determination—a will—to clear his name.

Blended in with this profound urge for vindication was a second catalyst toward activism: a philosophy of life that exalted practical achievement. If Hoover had spent two terms in the White House and retired to popular acclaim in 1937, it is quite likely that he still would have been an amazingly enterprising former president. An autobiographical statement that he composed sometime during World War I helps to explain why. "There is little importance to men's lives," he wrote, "except the accomplishments they leave posterity. . . . When all is said and done accomplishment is all that counts." For Hoover, life was not meant for idle talk or solipsistic leisure. His physical aversion to passivity was matched by his creed. Moreover, for him the most definable form of accomplishment was the creation or administration of what he called "tangible institutions." Between 1933 and 1964 three institutions in particular became the beneficiaries of his labors: the Hoover Institution at Stanford University, the Boys' Clubs of America movement, and, toward the end, the Herbert Hoover Presidential Library. Upon each he left a perdurable imprint; each in a way conferred upon him the secular immortality that I think he craved.

In 1920 Hoover remarked that "words without action are the assassins of idealism." This statement, I think, reveals the third volitional wellspring of his post-presidential behavior. He ordered his life not only by a philosophy of achievement but by a self-conscious ethic of benefaction. It was not enough for him to do well; from an early point in his life he yearned and strove to do good. As he told a friend before World War I, "Just making money isn't enough." It was one more bar to complacency and quietism. In the mid-1930s Hoover's brother Theodore estimated that Herbert had given away more than one-half of his profits for benevolent purposes over the years. He did not change his ways later on. Thus in 1944 he deeded to Stanford University his magnificent home on campus; the mansion is now the official residence of Stanford's president. Thus he committed countless hours to philanthropic and educational endeavors. All his benefactions cannot be catalogued here, but the point is clear. Undergirding his ceaseless activity was an impulse to perform good works, a desire raised in his mind to the level of an ethical imperative. One cannot understand his perpetual restlessness without taking this motivation into account.

From Hoover's kaleidoscopic ex-presidency, then, we may adduce this formula. If you wish to be a model of a modern former president, you should: live a long life; be blessed with excellent health and superabundant energy; have a source of income that frees you for public service; have a far-flung legion of friends willing to labor in your behalf; feel a passionate need to justify your record before your countrymen and posterity; have a philosophy of life that imbues in you a consuming desire to achieve, to build great institutions that will survive you, and to serve your fellow men and women unstintingly. And one thing more: You should possess an utter unwillingness to fade away.

Follow this formula, and it may be said of you what we may now conclude about Herbert Hoover. He secured his place in history the old-fashioned way: He *earned* it.

Former Presidents Herbert Hoover and Harry S. Truman
at the opening of the Truman Library.

III

MR. PRESIDENT—
MR. CITIZEN

Truman used these years to do things he had not been able to do before, which is why, I think, his post-presidential years were altogether the happiest time of his life, and in many ways, the most successful part of his life. "He is just so happy," one of his neighbors said, "it makes me happy just being around him." And the country, seeing the stories in *Life* magazine and other publications, began to feel that way as well.

What are the lessons of Harry Truman's life after he left the White House? His high visibility while he had been president and the many networks of public activity in which he became involved made it impossible, as long as he was physically able, for him to retire from view. . . . Truman served his country in important ways during his post-presidential years by contributing to the political process and by being a public educator. He did not need a seat in Congress or on a federal commission to do this, and the same has been true of later former presidents.

—David McCullough

—Donald R. McCoy

The Man of Independence
Harry S. Truman in Retirement

DAVID McCULLOUGH

Harry Truman arrived home from Washington on a cold night in January 1953. He expected there might be some turnout to welcome him, but he was totally amazed—overjoyed—by what happened. Ten thousand people came down to the Independence railroad depot to welcome the Trumans home. It was for him, and certainly for Mrs. Truman, the most heartwarming reception of their lives. "Well Harry, this makes it all worth it," Mrs. Truman said.

The next morning, when Mr. Truman was asked by the correspondent Ray Shearer what he intended to do first, now that he was back home, the president said, "I'm going to take the grips up to the attic." And with that famous line began one of the most interesting periods of Truman's life and one of the most interesting post-presidential careers of all.

Harry Truman lived seventy years of his life in Jackson County, Missouri. He was a senator in Washington, then a president for eighteen years in all, but most of his life was set in Jackson County, Missouri: this fact is essential to understanding Harry Truman.

He once said, "I tried never to forget who I was, where I came from, and where I would go back to." And unlike Herbert Hoover or Dwight Eisenhower, Harry Truman went back to his home town to live after his presidency. Contrary to what Thomas Wolfe said, Harry Truman was able to "go home again." He went home to stay and he loved it.

It was there, of course, that he built his library, and he was at his desk at the library, usually six days a week for nine years, a longer period than he was president. Indeed, for about nine years, the most memorable exhibit on display at the library was Truman himself.

He enjoyed being home, his morning walks, visits with neighbors; he enjoyed the library; most important, he enjoyed being Harry Truman. His vitality was what people who knew him best talked about. Dean Acheson wrote about it; Clark Clifford commented on it; the people who live next door to the Truman house talk about it still. That vitality was both infectious and gave the country a sense of the former president that they welcomed, his popularity growing steadily in these years.

Someone once said that Theodore Roosevelt's greatest gift to his country was Theodore himself: his personality, his approach to life, his response to problems and to being an American. This, I think, is also particularly true of Harry Truman in his post-presidential years, even though he performed no official public role. Being home again, being the Man of Independence in those years, he was performing one of the most important roles he could have chosen.

Truman returned to Independence with no Secret Service agents, no secretaries, no pension, no salary, not a penny of expense money. As a colonel in the Army Reserve he did draw a pension of $119.32 a month. Eventually, after 1958, a federal pension would provide him with $25,000 a year, plus $50,000 for office expenses. But among the major reasons the Trumans went back to 219 North Delaware Street in 1953 was because they could not afford to do anything else. They moved back into the Wallace house—as it's still known by old residents of Independence, Bess Truman's mother's house—just as they had after they were married. In 1913, when Truman was twenty-nine and still courting Bess Wallace, he wrote, "It seems like a hollow week if I don't arrive at 219 North Delaware at least one day in it." Well, he spent the rest of his life there.

Truman used these years to do things he had not been able to do before, which is chiefly why, I think, his post-presidential years were altogether the happiest time of his life and, in many ways, the most successful part of his life. "He is so happy," one of his neighbors said, "it makes me happy just being around him." And much of the country, seeing the stories in *Life* magazine and other publications, began to feel that way as well.

He went traveling as he had never done before. He went to Hawaii; he went to Europe twice; he saw London for the first time. He visited Churchill at Chartwell and received an honorary degree at Oxford—quite a thing, he said, for a man from Independence, Missouri. He played Mozart's piano at Salzburg and he saw the Colosseum in Rome and the Parthenon in Athens and toured monuments in Italy with— of all people—Henry Luce.

Back home, he helped Thomas Hart Benton paint part of the sky in an upper corner of the Benton mural at the Truman Library. In white tie and tails, he conducted the Kansas City Philharmonic Orchestra playing John Philip Sousa's "Stars and Stripes Forever."

He was driving his own car again—and how he loved to drive an automobile! He had no hobbies or conventional recreation; he never learned to play golf or tennis; he did not know how to dance. Driving the car, reading, and playing the piano were his pastimes, and, as he said, enjoying an occasional "H_2O flavored with bourbon." Once he was stopped for his driving on the Pennsylvania Turnpike. The state policeman who pulled him over said he was cutting in front of other cars every time he passed. The policeman asked Mr. Truman to please be more careful in the future.

Harry Truman voiced opinions on everything, and some were regrettable. The contents of the interviews with Merle Miller that eventually became the book *Plain Speaking* are at times intemperate, silly, and inaccurate, but they are vintage Truman in the post-presidential years. He was called the "common man" and he never saw any reason to think that was something to be ashamed of. Jake Arvey, the Chicago political leader and lawyer, once remarked that Harry Truman never thought he needed to look up to any man or down on any man.

On the topic of pomp and circumstance, there is this memorable entry in Truman's diary: "I never thought that God gives a damn about pomp and circumstance, gold crowns, jeweled breast plates and ancestral background. When the gates of heaven are reached by the shades of the earthbound, the rank and riches enjoyed on this planet won't be of value. Some of our grandees will have to do a lot of explaining on how they got that way. I wish I could hear their alibis. I can't, for the probabilities are that I'll be thinking up some for myself."

Most importantly, I think Harry Truman set a modern ethic for presidential retirement. This was a man without private resources. The publication of his memoirs was a financial disappointment. He did receive some money by selling off the old family farm, some 200 acres out in Grandview, Missouri, that was, to his great heartbreak I am sure, turned into a shopping center. The old farmhouse is there still, nicely restored, but surrounded by gasoline stations and fast-food restaurants.

He wrote, "I could never lend myself to any transaction, however respectable, that would commercialize on the prestige and the dignity of the office of the president." And he meant what he said. He took no fees for lobbying or writing letters or making phone calls. He never lent his name to any corporate undertaking; he accepted no "consulting" fees.

At this point in his life, this happiest of former presidents began what was, for him, a unique experience—a close relationship with a close male friend. There was now someone with whom he could correspond, someone to whom he wrote letters such as he had not written to anyone other than the women in his life: his wife, his mother, his daughter, and his sister. The friend was the most unexpected of people—Dean Acheson. What an odd couple, we might say: the elegant, Edwardian Acheson and the plain-speaking president from Missouri. Truman and Acheson corresponded back and forth for years and their letters are revealing, touching, humorous, and very human.

The two men had more in common than one might think. Staunch patriots, both came from small towns, and both had quick, retentive minds and the courage of their convictions. Both men essentially wanted to do the right thing and believed fervently that unless the government—unless the country—was led by people of responsibility and ability, it could all well go down the drain.

"I wish I could sit and talk with you for an hour, or thirty minutes, or even for five minutes. My morale would go up one hundred percent," Truman wrote to Dean Acheson. "Do you suppose any president of the United States ever had two such men with him as you and the General?" he says at another point. He is referring here, of course, to George C. Marshall, the American he admired above all others. "You have been a tower of strength to me in all my trials and tribulations," he wrote to Acheson. On receiving the president's memoirs, Acheson wrote that "this book will always be the President to me. He will also be the man of unflinching courage and integrity and deepest warmth, simplicity and loyalty with whom the great association of my life was lived."

Acheson invited Truman to Yale as a Chubb Fellow who would lecture to the students for several days. In reply Truman wrote a handsome and revealing compliment: "I would be proud to appear anywhere with you from Yale to 1908 Main Street in Kansas City." The address (1908 Main Street) referred to the former office of Tom Pendergast, the notorious political boss of Kansas City and Truman's early mentor.

Truman once remarked that he would have given anything to have had a Yale education. So here, on the one hand, was all that Acheson and Yale represented; and on the other hand, the Pendergast past he had had to carry with him all through his political life. But he now told Dean Acheson that he would even stand in front of 1908 Main if Acheson would go with him.

"I hope that you and I will never lose contact," Truman wrote—something that, as far as I know, he never said to anybody else, never wrote in this way to any other man. For all of his male occupations in life—the Army, politics— he had had no close male confidant, not until Acheson in the years after the White House.

Acheson wrote to Thomas Bergen, then the Master at Timothy Dwight College at Yale: "Mr. Truman is deeply interested in and very good with the young. His point of view is fresh, eager, confident. He has learned the hard way, but he has learned a lot. He believes in his fellow man and he believes that with will and courage and some intelligence the future is manageable. I should want Mr. Truman to be received at Yale with honor, with simplicity, not as a show, not with controversy, not as a lecturer in a field which I do not believe is yet a discipline, but as one who could, if in some way we were able to wire for spirit, give our under-graduates more sense of what their lives are worth than anyone I know." It was the *spirit* that mattered above all, and it was still flowing strong.

Harry Truman came home to Independence as the former president who had been to Potsdam with Stalin and Churchill, who had launched the Truman Doctrine and the Marshall Plan, who recognized the new nation of Israel, who had established the Central Intelligence Agency and the National Security Council, who dropped the atomic bomb and made the decision to proceed with the hydrogen bomb, who had established the Air Force as a separate service and who set up the Department of Defense, who had led us to war in Korea and fired General Douglas MacArthur, and who had done more for civil rights than any president since Lincoln. Among other things.

But when he came home, it was to face the appraisal again, of course, of the people of Independence, including a good number of Republicans. (And Truman's standing with the country then was, it should be remembered, at an all-time low.) One of his neighbors was a man named Henry Bundschu, a life-long Republican, who made this comment after observing how Mr. Truman conducted himself: "I used to say that Harry Truman lived around the corner from me; now there isn't a day goes by that I don't tell myself 'you live around the corner from Harry Truman and don't you ever forget it.'"

"Harry feels square with the world," an old Missouri friend said of him in his last years. "He feels that he gave it his best."

I believe that high among the reasons that the post-presidential years were such a satisfactory time for him was just this: the feeling that he had done his best. It was time for him to retire, not unlike Cincinnatus, the Roman hero—and among Truman's life-long heroes—who came back from war after having led his country to victory and then returned home to the plow. "Hello old farmer," said Speaker Sam Rayburn and Harry Truman when they greeted one another over the telephone. Truman liked to speak of himself as a retired farmer—and yes, in the tradition of the retired farmer, he was now living in town.

He took his early morning walks until he was too old to go any more. A regular companion on these walks was Thomas Melton, the minister of the First Presbyterian Church on Pleasant Street, the same church where Bess Wallace and Harry Truman had met as children in Sunday school. Reverend Melton and President Truman would usually take the same route each morning, passing by Mr. Bundschu's house, in front of which stands what must be the biggest Ginko tree in all of Missouri, an enormous, spectacular tree. Reverend Melton told me that when they passed the tree, Mr. Truman would speak to it.

"Speak to the tree?" I asked.

"Yes, every morning."

"What did he say?"

"He said, 'You're doing a good job.'"

Many people would have said the same of Mr. Truman in his post-presidential years.

"Be Yourself":
Harry S. Truman
as a Former President

DONALD R. MCCOY

Harry S. Truman had one of the longest ex-presidencies in American history, surviving for almost twenty years after leaving office, a period exceeded only by Herbert Hoover, John Adams, Martin Van Buren, and Millard Fillmore. Truman's last eight years were, sadly, a period of steady and even steep physical decline. Therefore, this essay will focus largely on the approximately dozen years immediately after he left office, a time of strenuous activity for him.

Looking at what Harry Truman did then might provide some answers to what former presidents should do. After the cheers he heard upon leaving Washington and returning home in 1953 had ceased, he had to face life as "Mr. Citizen," as he called it, instead of as Mr. President. His activities fell roughly into four categories: family man; wage earner; educator; and political figure.

I will not say much about Harry Truman the family man. He continued to be a devoted husband to his best friend, the "Boss," Bess Truman, and to dote upon his only child, Margaret. Eventually, he received dividends in his son-in-law, Clifton Daniel, whom Truman treated much like the son he never had, and in his four grandsons to whom he was an affectionate grandfather. He also had close relations with other members of the Truman clan. In short, his personal life was rich after the White House years.

Truman's role as wage earner initially promised to be difficult. Except for an inheritance and some perquisites as a former senator and retired National Guard colonel, he had little with which to provide for his retirement years. These would be expensive years, considering what would be expected of him as a political leader and as, so to say, history on the hoof. As early as 1952 Truman began seeking respectable post-presidential employment and considered various offers of work. This was frustrating, for he was determined to accept nothing that would demean his name and former high office. The suitable pickings were few, but they did, before long, provide enough for him to live a relatively affluent life. Most important as a source of income was the $600,000 he received for the publication of his memoirs. Truman also earned money making television appearances, giving lectures, and writing another book, *Mr. Citizen*, and occasional newspaper articles. In 1958 he began benefiting from legislation that provided pensions and expense allowances for former presidents.

Harry Truman took his role as an educator seriously. Central to filling this role was his concern that his White House files be saved for posterity. As early as 1949, he began placing some historical materials in the National Archives. In 1950 he successfully initiated legislation to permit that agency to receive the papers of the chief executive and other high federal officials. That same year, though, Truman decided to follow Franklin D. Roosevelt's precedent and establish his own presidential library. His chief purpose, as he stated in 1954, was that his library would "belong to the people of the United States. My papers will be the property of the people and be accessible to them. And this is as it should be. The papers of the Presidents are among the most valuable sources of material for history. They ought to be preserved, and they ought to be used." By the time the Harry

S. Truman Library opened its doors in 1957, $1.8 million
had been privately contributed to its construction. Truman
raised $1 million of this amount, largely by giving lectures.
It was his broader intention that the library become a center
for education on the American presidency through research,
conferences, lectures, and museum functions — a goal that
has been splendidly achieved. Truman and his associates
were also important in spurring the enactment, with the
cooperation of the Eisenhower administration, of the Presidential Libraries Act of 1955, which authorized the National
Archives and Records Service to receive, administer, and
maintain presidential materials and privately built structures
like the Truman Library to hold them. Thus, a major type
of institution for historical research and public education,
the presidential library, was made a permanent and expand-
ing part of the national scene.

There were related results from Truman's concern for the
preservation of presidential papers for research. With his
support in 1954, a few of his former aides pressed the
government to publish the essential documentation of his
presidency. Again there was a community of interest with
the Eisenhower administration. The result was the establishment in 1957 of the publication project known as the *Public
Papers of the Presidents*, which has been a boon to private
and government researchers. The first volume pertained to
Eisenhower and appeared in 1958; the first one dealing with
Truman was published in 1961. Harry Truman was also
interested in making the papers of the earlier presidents that
were housed in the Library of Congress more available for
use. Therefore, in June 1957 he testified before a congressional committee in support of a bill to fund the microfilming
and indexing of these collections for public sale: the legislation was adopted.

Not surprisingly, political commentary was the most

prominent of Truman's post-presidential activities. He could hardly avoid it, given how often newsmen and his fellow Democrats would ask him what he thought about this, that, and what not. Moreover, he believed he had a duty to protect the interests of his party and country and a responsibility to defend his record. When the Republican National Committee proposed that his party be renamed the Democrat party. Truman responded that this was fine, "Providing, of course, they let us change the name of their party to the Publican Party. You know, in the Bible those publicans and big-money boys didn't come off too well." His poor relationship with Dwight D. Eisenhower, which seems petty in retrospect, fortunately, began to mend in the 1960s.

In his memoirs and in *Mr. Citizen*, Truman spent much time defending his administration's policies as well as commenting on history and government. These themes were also heard in the many lectures he gave. Perhaps the question Truman was most often asked was why he authorized the use of the atomic bomb against Japan in 1945. His answer was direct: "It was the right thing to do, and I always do the right thing."

Of special concern were his proposals for what former presidents should do. Truman thought that they should be involved in special services and activities—like Herbert Hoover's work in international relief and in the reorganization of the executive branch. Truman also proposed that former presidents should be nonvoting members of the House of Representatives and the Senate. After he left office he took part in legislative matters by testifying before House and Senate committees. He also reinforced an important precedent relating to executive privilege by refusing to comply with a subpoena from the House Un-American Activities Committee in 1953.

Truman believed that former presidents should speak their

minds, and so he did often. One example was his comment on the evangelist Billy Graham. Truman said, "He's gone off the beam. . . . He claims he's a friend of all the presidents, but he was never a friend of mine when I was president. I just don't go for people like that. All he's interested in is getting his name in the paper." On official matters, however, Truman thought former presidents should speak more carefully than when they had been in the White House. He was discreet about commenting on foreign policy in order to avoid embarrassing his successors in their conduct of foreign affairs and to encourage bipartisanship in such matters. His discretion also applied to domestic issues with respect to his Democratic successors as president. When John F. Kennedy was president, Truman once told reporters that he disapproved of the administration's plans for deficit spending. The White House asked him not to comment along this line, and, as a loyal Democrat, he complied with this request.

Harry Truman took an active part in the affairs of his party between the 1952 and 1960 elections, seeking to strengthen its political appeal in various ways. This sometimes put him on a collision course with other Democratic leaders, especially Adlai E. Stevenson, the party's 1952 standard-bearer. Truman had not been pleased with Stevenson's management of the 1952 campaign. Yet in July 1955 he asked Stevenson to announce for the 1956 Democratic presidential nomination. When Stevenson demurred, Truman's view of him as indecisive was reinforced, and the former president supported Governor Averell Harriman of New York for the nomination. Nevertheless, Stevenson won a smashing first-ballot nomination victory at the 1956 Democratic convention.

After their party's 1956 presidential election defeat, Stevenson and Truman joined together to establish the Democratic Advisory Council in order to heal the party's wounds and to fashion a vigorous and appealing program. The council's work helped to ease intraparty strife and in effect reaffirmed Democratic support for Truman's views on foreign policy and Stevenson's less liberal views on domestic issues. This also had considerable influence on the Kennedy administration's policies, in part because one-third of the 275 leaders involved in the Democratic Advisory Council served in that administration.

The council did not resolve differences among Democrats over whom to nominate for president in 1960, and Truman played a role in the jockeying for the nomination. He was thoroughly discouraged with Stevenson, and the former president still had bite. As Stevenson described him in 1958, Truman as a speaker "was pungent, sharp and politically effective, for the multitude, as long as he was giving 'em hell." The two Democratic stalwarts were personally cordial to each other and in public made flattering remarks about one another.

Stevenson, though, had to restrain himself from indicating what he really thought of Truman on one public occasion when they were together. He yearned to tell the story—but did not—about the sentencing of a Kentucky moonshiner for the tenth time. The "exasperated judge said, . . . 'you've caused this court more trouble than anyone ever did before; have you anything to say before I sentence you again.' 'Only this judge; that *you've* caused me just as much trouble as I have caused you!'" Stevenson would have added, "and thats (*sic*) the way I feel about our beloved guest of honor: HST."

Beginning in 1959, Truman began booming his fellow Missourian, Senator Stuart Symington, for the 1960 Democratic presidential nomination; but he also would accept the candidacy of Senate Majority Leader Lyndon B. Johnson. Neither of them had much of a chance. As Truman wrote in June 1960, "It looks as if this Convention has been packed against both of them," and, he might have added, with no regret, against Stevenson. The front runner was John F. Kennedy, whom Truman opposed. As he quipped, "It's not the pope I fear but the pop." But it was more than that, as he wrote to his daughter: "Old man Joe Kennedy has spent over 4 million dollars to buy the nomination for his son! Then the anti-pope and the Lutherans, Baptists and Methodists, with the Presbyterians and Campbellites will beat him."

Nevertheless, after Kennedy was nominated for president, Truman loyally campaigned for him as he had for Stevenson in 1956. According to the Associated Press, Truman said that the Republican presidential nominee, Richard M. Nixon, "never told the truth in his life." The former president was not sure that he had said this, but he believed that no one could challenge the truth of the idea. "After all, I didn't call him an S.O.B. because he insists he's a self-made man! You all know that's a lie—Eisenhower made him!" In any case, Truman's efforts in the 1960 campaign were richly rewarded. Not only did Kennedy win, but equally important he defeated a man whom Truman could never forgive for having called him a traitor in 1952.

With Kennedy's election as president, Truman's political role diminished, although he was still available for speeches and consultation. In 1962 he traveled to Idaho to encourage unity among that state's badly divided Democrats. The Pocatello Chamber of Commerce named him "Chief 'Give 'em Hell' Harry" and issued a brochure that included a photograph of him in Indian headdress. Thinking of a similar photograph of Calvin Coolidge, he wrote, "And I've laughed at a former President." More publicized was Truman's sally into California that year to speak against Richard Nixon's ill-starred candidacy for governor. It is not known exactly what Truman said, but apparently he did not refer to Nixon as "squirrelhead," as he did in private. Truman's notes indicate that he only called Nixon a "mean, nasty fellow," adding that he "couldn't get into the front door of the White House. Now he's trying to sneak in over the transom."

Truman's activities diminished between 1964 and his death in 1972. He endorsed Lyndon Johnson's candidacy for president in 1964. He represented the United States at the funeral of King Paul of Greece and was invited to speak to the United States Senate. In October he seriously injured himself in a fall in his bathroom. After that he was less and less the Harry Truman of old. In 1965, though, he watched with pleasure as President Johnson signed the Medicare legislation at the Truman Library. He supported the American intervention into Vietnam. Truman endorsed the Humphrey-Muskie ticket in 1968. When the two Democratic nominees visited him, his advice, at least to Senator Edmund Muskie, was "Tell the truth" and "Be yourself." Truman seldom saw visitors or was seen in public after that. In December 1972 he died.

What are the lessons of Harry Truman's life after he left the White House? His high visibility while he had been president and the many networks of public activity in which he had become involved made it impossible, as long as he was physically able, for him to retire from view. As he said, "After you've served as President of the United States, you can never again expect to be a plain, ordinary citizen." Truman served his country in important ways during his post-presidential years by contributing to the political process and by being a public educator. He did this rarely on invitation from the government. Given the nature of the media and political spheres and the public's insatiable curiosity about celebrities, Truman had abundant opportunities to make known his views. He did not need a seat in Congress or on a federal commission to do this, and the same has been true of later former presidents.

So far these self-defined post-presidential activities have worked reasonably well for former presidents and for the nation, a proposition with which Harry Truman and Herbert Hoover would probably agree. After all, they both experienced intense criticism in the presidency and afterward; yet they reaped great satisfactions and contributed significantly to the country they had once served as chief executive.

Former President Dwight D. Eisenhower at the Hoover Library.

IV

AN OLD SOLDIER
RETIRES

Overall, in his role as a former president, Eisenhower carried out his ceremonial functions with his usual grace and charm. He wrote a two-volume set of memoirs that remain the starting point for any serious student of politics and statecraft in the 1950s, as well as a delightful set of informal memoirs. As the guiding spirit who set the tone for his presidential library, he was a perfect model—one all of his successors would do well to follow.

As a keen student of history, Eisenhower made better use of his ex-presidency than most of his predecessors. More than a few of his skeptics have now acknowledged that the American voter was right to like Ike. And had it not been for the Twenty-second Amendment, they would have extended his lease on the White House for as long as he wanted.

—Stephen E. Ambrose

—Steve Neal

At Ease:
Dwight D. Eisenhower
in Retirement

STEPHEN E. AMBROSE

On January 20, 1961, following the inaugural ceremonies of John F. Kennedy, Dwight and Mamie Eisenhower sneaked away to a farewell lunch with his cabinet. In so doing, Eisenhower later wrote, they made "a fantastic discovery. We were free—as only private citizens in a democratic nation can be free."

After lunch, they drove to their retirement home in Gettysburg. By special, unprecedented action on Kennedy's part, Eisenhower was retaining his Secret Service bodyguard as a driver for two weeks. When they got to the farm, Ike hopped out of the car to open the gate. In twenty years, it was the first personal physical need that he had taken care of himself.

He did not know how to pay tolls at the automatic lanes on the turnpikes; he had forgotten how to type; he could not mix frozen orange juice or adjust a TV picture. He did not even know how to place a telephone call. The last time he had done so, in 1941, he told the operator the number he wanted. On the evening of January 20, he picked up the receiver to call his son John. There was no operator, only a buzz. He yelled into the phone; no response. He clicked the button a dozen times; no response. He shouted at the agent: "Come show me how you work this goddamn thing." "Oh, so that's how you do it!"

Delighted and fascinated, he placed call after call. He rather thought he might enjoy this business of learning to cope with the modern world.

He was a private citizen. After a full one-half century in its service, the nation had finally allowed him to retire. He was free. Well, not quite. He was the first president since Teddy Roosevelt who, when he retired, retained the admiration and affection of a majority of his countrymen, the only one since Roosevelt who could have been easily reelected. So his position was special, and it imposed on him duties and obligations. He was the nation's elder statesman, which meant that his views on foreign and domestic policies should carry weight. Because the Republicans had lost the 1960 election, he was titular leader of the Party. But because he was seventy years old, and because the Twenty-second Amendment prevented him from running for the presidency again, he had to use persuasion and logic, in place of power or the threat of taking power, to influence events.

He was in a delicate position and so were his successors: Kennedy, Johnson, and Nixon. Kennedy and Johnson wanted his public approval of their foreign policies; Nixon wanted his support for another Republican nomination. Because Eisenhower was ambiguous in all three cases, he found himself being pushed and pulled and tugged in different directions.

Worse, he found that his power to influence events was limited at best. The Republican party wanted him for his fundraising ability, and he made various appearances and speeches for that cause. But as the Party drifted toward the right and the Goldwater nomination, he found that these politicians did not want his advice. In the summer of 1962, Eisenhower tried to take the party leadership away from the Old Guard–dominated Republican National Committee. He organized the Republican Citizens Committee, designed in his words to serve as "a bridge between the Republican Party and the Independents and the dissatisfied Democrats" by moving to the middle-of-the-road. To his dismay he discovered that the Old Guard would rather control a minority party than share power in a majority party. The Republican Citizens Committee died.

He was equally unsuccessful in shaping the long-term future of the government. He wanted a series of constitutional changes and spoke often for them. They included a line-item veto, a four-year term for the House of Representatives, and a two-thirds vote of the Senate to reject a presidential appointee to the executive branch. All would have added to the power of the Oval Office; Congress greeted each with a yawn.

Meanwhile, his health took a pounding. He suffered four heart attacks in his retirement and underwent a couple of operations. He spent the last year of his life in a hospital.

There were compensations. He loved his home in Gettysburg and loved playing at being a farmer. His time with Mamie was precious to him. He thoroughly enjoyed his winters in the California desert. He did a lot of traveling, always a lifelong passion. His grandchildren were a special source of joy. Writing his presidential memoirs and the informal autobiography *At Ease* gave him solid, satisfying work to do.

He enjoyed being interviewed by historians. Once, after a long day of such interviews, he sighed with weariness as he mixed cocktails for himself and his brother Milton. "Tough day," Milton said with sympathy. "Yes," Ike agreed, "but it would be worse to be forgotten." He was not unaware that through his memoirs and the interviews, he was helping establish his place in history—something that mattered very much to him.

Thus he expressed keen interest and delight in the establishment of the Eisenhower Library and Museum in Abilene. In contrast to some of his successors, he felt he had nothing to be ashamed of, and much to be proud of, in his career, so he ordered that the full uncensored record be made available to scholars as soon as possible. He also cooperated fully in a project Milton set up at Johns Hopkins University: the publication of his papers in a multivolume series. The more people knew about him, he believed, the more they would admire him. He was right.

On his deathbed, he said that he had always loved his country. He had spent his life in the service of the nation. A full fifty years, from 1911 to 1961. He could not help but fret over the developments of the 1960s. He tried to influence them through occasional public pronouncements, but because he was a soldier in whom the doctrine of support for the commander in chief was embedded, he did not want to be publicly critical of the president. Indeed, he did all he could to be supportive, especially in foreign affairs.

In private, to friends, he complained bitterly about Kennedy's "careless spending, his complete lack of interest in the soundness of the dollar," and about Kennedy's "buildup of the military, the space scientists and armament industries." He feared that "this combination can be so powerful and the military machine so big it just has to be used," but he kept his thoughts to himself.

Following the Bay of Pigs disaster, Kennedy invited Eisenhower to Camp David for consultation. Ike asked if "before you approved this plan did you have everybody in front of you debating the thing so you got the pros and cons yourself and then make your decision?" Kennedy confessed that he had not. Ike thought him "a little bewildered." He asked why on earth Kennedy had not provided air cover for the invasion. Kennedy replied, "My advice was that we must try to keep our hands from showing in the affair." Astounded,

Ike snapped back, "Mr. President, how could you expect the world to believe that we had nothing to do with it? . . . I believe there is only one thing to do when you go into this kind of thing. It must be a success."

Eisenhower advised Kennedy to revive the National Security Council and consult fully with it in the future. He opposed going to the moon. He consistently told Kennnedy to get tough with the Russians; as one example he urged the president to tear down the Berlin Wall the day it went up. He was furious when Kennedy, who did not consult him during the Cuban missile crisis, promised not to invade Cuba in return for Khrushchev's removal of the missiles. Eisenhower told John McCone, head of the Central Intelligence Agency; "We owe it to ourselves to (a) First, *make certain* all missiles are gone [through on-site inspections], and (b) To assert our right to take such action, at any time, against Castro as would assure protection against subversion, sabotage, etc." But to Ike's disgust, Kennedy did nothing.

One noteworthy aspect of Ike's advice was how belligerent he had become. When he was in office, Eisenhower had received a constant stream of advice—whenever there was a crisis with the Communists, whether it was in Korea or Vietnam or Formosa or Hungary or Berlin—to get tough, to stand up to Khrushchev, to use whatever force was necessary. He had consistently rejected such advice. But out of office, he was much tougher, much more willing to go the whole route, than he had been when the decision was his responsibility.

Kennedy's assassination put Lyndon Johnson in power. Eisenhower had always been contemptuous of Johnson, but once Johnson took the oath of office, he did what he could to rally behind the new leader. Still, he could not restrain himself in his private comments. "Johnson," he told one caller, "is unreliable and has no moral courage whatsoever."

When former Treasury Secretary George Humphrey expressed doubts about Johnson's backbone, Ike snapped, "He never had any."

In 1964, critics were saying that it was Eisenhower who lacked backbone because of his refusal to endorse a Republican candidate to stop the Barry Goldwater movement. It seemed inconceivable that Ike would stand aside while Goldwater returned the Republican party to the principles of Warren Harding, thereby repudiating Eisenhower's middle-of-the-road, moderate policies; but stand aside he did. He appeared particularly inept when he urged Governor William Scranton of Pennsylvania to enter the race and then withheld a public endorsement. It seemed that he cared more about his position as Grand Old Man of the Grand Old Party than he did for the Party itself.

When Goldwater won the nomination and proclaimed that "extremism in the defense of liberty is no vice! Moderation in the pursuit of justice is no virtue!" Ike protested privately that the statement "would seem to say that the end always justifies the means. The whole American system refutes that idea." But in public he pledged to "do my best to support Goldwater."

Never had Ike appeared so bumbling or ineffective. Never had he gone so far in appeasing the Old Guard. Never was he so roundly criticized. He was, however, in an awkward position. With Nixon resolutely on the sidelines, the only man who had a reasonable chance of stopping Goldwater was Rockefeller, who was anathema to Eisenhower. So he endorsed Goldwater, and during the campaign he made a TV special at his farm. Goldwater sat with him on the lawn, where they discussed the "silly notion" that Goldwater was a right-wing extremist. It was a dismal performance, about which the less said the better. In November, Goldwater and the Republican party suffered a humiliating defeat.

After the election, public life in the United States was dominated by Lyndon Johnson and the war in Vietnam. Johnson desperately wanted Ike's support and his advice. As Johnson began to escalate the war, he started the practice of writing or calling Eisenhower before every significant act. Although Johnson's letters to Eisenhower were so full of overblown praise and gratitude as to be obsequious and phony, Johnson was quite sincere in his requests for Ike's counsel, to which he gave great weight. He was obviously aware of how valuable Ike's public support of his Vietnam policy could be to him, and he was not above using Eisenhower for his own purposes in this regard; but the record makes it clear that as Johnson made his crucial decisions on the conduct of the war in Vietnam, he both sought and was influenced by Ike's advice. It is equally true that Ike's advice was consistently hawkish and that the main thrust of his criticism of Johnson on Vietnam—insofar as he was critical rather than supportive—was that Johnson was not doing enough.

On February 17, 1965, in the Cabinet Room at the White House, Eisenhower met for two and one-half hours with Johnson, Robert McNamara, McGeorge Bundy, and Generals Earle Wheeler and Andrew Goodpaster. The notes of the meeting remained top secret until August 1982, when they were declassified. Again and again during the meeting, Ike urged more air strikes. Goodpaster's notes read: "He said that in his opinion, these retaliation actions have helped the situation a great deal. However, he felt it is now important to shift to a campaign of pressure. Targets should be struck north of the border. He thought such strikes could be well justified before the world."

Taking up the possibility of Chinese or Soviet intervention, Ike said, "if they threaten to intervene we should pass the word back to them to take care lest dire results occur to them. [He thought] we should let them know now what we are seeking to do and that we would act against them if necessary."

As to the possibility of negotiations with North Vietnam, he "felt that negotiation from weakness is likely to lead only into deceit and vulnerability, which could be disastrous to us. [He advised] not to negotiate from a position of weakness."

McNamara asked for comments on escalation on the ground. Ike replied that "we should be sure that the enemy does not lack an appreciation of our stamina and determination to keep nations free by whatever means required." He thought that if they find we are ready, they will not come in great strength. He hoped "it would not be necessary to use the six to eight divisions mentioned, but if it should be necessary, so be it." In Eisenhower's view, the "greatest danger is that the Chinese get the idea that we will go just so far and no further in terms of the level of war we would conduct. That would be the beginning of the end, since they would know all they had to do was go further than we do."

Thus Eisenhower, at the critical moment, told Johnson to go all-out for victory. In 1954, however, Eisenhower had rejected similar advice with the comment that the jungles of Southeast Asia would just swallow up our divisions. It also illustrates how easy it is to give go-for-broke advice when you do not have to make the decision and give the order yourself.

Beginning in April 1965, Johnson sent Goodpaster to Palm Desert or Gettysburg on a biweekly basis to give Ike detailed briefings on what was happening and to seek his advice. The advice was to "untie Westmoreland's hands." Goodpaster's notes record that Eisenhower "strongly recommended getting rid of restrictions and delaying procedures." At a June 16 briefing, Eisenhower commented, "We have now appealed to force in South Vietnam, and therefore we have got to win." He wanted Westmoreland unleashed and a general offensive started.

Through the summer of 1965, Ike remained extremely hawkish. He wanted to mine the harbor of Haiphong; he said, "We should not base our action on minimum needs, but should swamp the enemy with overwhelming force." As Johnson escalated on the ground, Ike told Goodpaster to tell him "there is no question about his [Eisenhower's] support for what the President is doing. He supports it strongly."

By the end of 1966, however, Ike was growing impatient. Johnson was always about a year and one-half too late, he told Nixon. In April 1967, Ike told Goodpaster to tell Johnson that "a course of 'gradualism' is bound to be ineffective." To make his point, he used one of his favorite examples: If a general sent a battalion to take a hill, he might get the hill, but would suffer heavy casualties in the process, whereas if he sent a division, the casualties would be minimal. But even if Johnson was sending battalions rather than divisions, at least he was proclaiming his resolution to stay the course, and on that basis Ike continued to support him.

But by July 1967, Eisenhower was increasingly frustrated. He advocated extreme action. He made a public call for Congress to declare war against North Vietnam and to give that war "first priority," meaning, above the War on Poverty. He said the country should "take any action to win," and when asked if he would draw the line at the use of nuclear weapons, replied, "I would not automatically preclude anything. When you appeal to force to carry out the policies of America abroad there is no court above you."

The growing antiwar movement bothered him considerably. He complained about the "whimperings and whinings from frustrated partisans." He complained about the "'kooks' and 'hippies' and all the rest that are talking about surrendering." But it was not just the kooks and hippies who wanted out, as he well knew. He told Goodpaster privately that many of his own friends "are talking in terms of discouragement. They say that nothing seems to be going well and that, perhaps, it would be better to get out of it than to continue."

Ike was having none of that. He got fully behind Johnson in a public relations campaign. In November 1967, he joined with Omar Bradley and Harry Truman to make a television broadcast from Gettysburg. The three old men urged the nation to not just stay the course but to go for victory. Eisenhower advocated an invasion of North Vietnam and hot pursuit into Cambodia and Laos.

His anger mounted as his advice was rejected and the situation grew worse. Early in 1968, in an article in *Reader's Digest*, he charged that "the current raucous confrontation goes far beyond honorable dissent." In language stronger than any he had used when he was president, Eisenhower charged that the antiwar movement "is rebellion, and it verges on treason."

Johnson flew to Palm Desert for a visit. Afterward, he wrote Eisenhower, "I could not resist dropping in to draw on the strength of your wisdom and friendship again. I will persevere, sustained by your support." But just weeks later, the Communists launched their Tet offensive, and Johnson did badly in the New Hampshire primary, and Senator Robert Kennedy entered the race against him.

Johnson had promised Ike he would stay the course, but shortly thereafter he went on national television to announce that he was halting the bombing of most of North Vietnam and that he was personally withdrawing from the presidential race. Ike was livid; his remarks about Johnson's cutting and running were scathing.

Thus did Eisenhower find his role as elder statesman to be frustrating and irritating. Johnson said he wanted Ike's advice, but after 1965 he did not take it. The doves simply ignored the former president. Ike's own friends found him increasingly irrelevant. To his annoyance, Ike found his own words quoted against his position, as commentators revived the things he had said in 1954 about the inadvisability of fighting a ground war in Vietnam.

The events seem to point to a simple and direct conclusion: A former president who tries to exert influence on critical and controversial issues is bound to be frustrated. The man in the White House, especially—but not only—if he belongs to the opposition party, will flatter the former president, cajole him, and use him; it is, however, all but inevitable that he will not really listen to him. Not that Ike was right on Vietnam in the mid-1960s; to the contrary, he was right in the mid-1950s when he had the power of decision.

Eisenhower had a happier experience in the campaign for the Republican nomination in 1968, although by no means did he play a decisive or even important role. His candidate was Nixon, and unlike 1960 he had no hesitancy about him. It was not so much that Nixon had gone up in his estimation—although he had—as it was a case of having no choice. The other contenders, Nelson Rockefeller, George Romney, and Ronald Reagan, were all unacceptable for various reasons; and in comparison to any Democratic candidate, Nixon was, in Ike's view, light-years ahead.

His commitment to Nixon was solidified by the courtship then going on between his grandson David and Nixon's daughter Julie. After some pressure from the family, Ike decided to break his self-serving and self-made rule to withhold endorsement of a candidate before the convention had chosen one. On July 15, when Nixon stopped in at Ward

Eight at Walter Reed Hospital for a conference, Ike told him of his decision. Nixon was naturally delighted, but being Nixon he found something to worry about.

Ike had told Nixon that he would make his endorsement public on the day the convention opened. Nixon objected that by then a number of favorite sons would have released their delegates so that they could cast their ballots for Nixon. Thus, Nixon told Eisenhower, "we face the distinct possibility that in the public mind the decision would have been made before your endorsement was announced." So he wanted an immediate endorsement. Two days later, Eisenhower did as Nixon wished. He released a statement saying he supported Nixon "because of my admiration of his personal qualities: his intellect, decisiveness, warmth, and above all, his integrity."

Eisenhower played no role in the campaign. He was far too weak and ill. After winning the election, Nixon brought his Cabinet appointees to Walter Reed to meet Ike. Henry Kissinger, who had indulged in typical academic sneering of President Eisenhower in the 1950s, was deeply impressed by how active Ike's mind was despite his physical condition. Ike urged Kissinger to protect Nixon from leaks, which was surely a case of asking the fox to guard the henhouse.

My own research has not yet uncovered any example of Nixon asking Eisenhower for his advice; the evidence is that he did not seek any—particularly on Vietnam. A good thing, too, as Nixon had decided even before he took office to retreat. Ike was old and sick; he died two months after Nixon's inaugural, so he could hardly have had an impact on the Nixon presidency.

Overall, in his role as a former president, Eisenhower carried out his ceremonial functions with his usual grace and charm. He wrote a two-volume set of memoirs that remain the starting point for any serious student of politics and statecraft of the 1950s as well as a delightful set of informal memoirs. As the guiding spirit who set the tone for his presidential library, he was a perfect model—one all his successors would do well to follow.

But as a man who wanted to have an impact on public policy, to be listened to, to have influence, he was a failure. It is not clear whether this failure was attributable to the fact that his immediate successors belonged to the opposition party, to the inappropriate nature of his advice, to the times being out of joint, or to the perennial fate of former presidents. You must judge for yourselves.

Everyone Liked Ike:
Dwight D. Eisenhower as a Former President

STEVE NEAL

In the summer of 1964, William F. Buckley, Jr., had a whimsical scheme to help his friend Barry Goldwater win the presidency. On the eve of the Republican national convention, Buckley advised Goldwater to choose former president Dwight D. Eisenhower as his running mate. Buckley was not a great admirer of the Eisenhower administration, which he had once scorned as socialistic; but the editor and founder of the *National Review* could read the numbers, and he knew that Eisenhower was still the most popular man in America.

There was no chance, of course, that Eisenhower would seriously consider such an invitation. In his private correspondence, Eisenhower would describe Goldwater as "nuts," and he disavowed his right-wing dogma. Goldwater was under no illusions that he was Ike's favorite candidate. And he also knew the former supreme allied commander well enough to know that he would never be relegated to second place on a national ticket.

For Dwight D. Eisenhower, retirement in the 1960s was a time of frustration. Because of the Twenty-second Amendment to the Constitution, which went into effect in the winter of 1951, he was the first person in American history to be legally barred from seeking the presidency after two terms in office. Without the shackles of the Twenty-second Amendment, which had been promoted by the Republican-controlled Eightieth Congress to block another FDR, there is not much doubt that Eisenhower would have sought a third term in 1960. Given his popularity and the peace and the prosperity of the times, there is also little doubt that Eisenhower would have been reelected. If he had maintained his vigor and health in a third term, it is within the realm of possibility that he might have attempted to have matched Roosevelt's record by winning a fourth term in 1964.

But in January 1961, Eisenhower went into a forced retirement. The most powerful man in the world in the 1950s and the supreme allied commander of the grand alliance in the 1940s was in the new role of private citizen in the 1960s. Since Eisenhower was considerably more popular than the Republican party, the loss of the White House was probably inevitable for the GOP in 1960. But Eisenhower considered the defeat of his vice president, Richard M. Nixon, in the 1960 presidential election, as nothing less than a repudiation of his administration. Ike told his son, John, that he might as well have "been having fun" during the previous eight years.

His regimen was not much different from that of other former presidents. He spoke out about constitutional issues, raised funds and campaigned for Republican candidates, took an active role in the development of his presidential library, and wrote his memoirs with a team of writers and editors. In 1964 he narrated a memorable television program, "D-Day Plus 20," from the beaches of Normandy with his friend Walter Cronkite. As a former president, Eisenhower became a familiar presence at the funerals of other major historical figures. In January 1965, he led the American delegation to London for the funeral of his wartime comrade Winston Churchill. Back home, he sat with other former presidents at the funerals of Sam Rayburn, Eleanor Roosevelt, and John F. Kennedy.

For Eisenhower, these somber occasions were a time for reflection, and past differences, at least for the moment, were put aside if not forgotten. Averell Harriman said later that his frosty relationship with Eisenhower thawed as they sat together on the Air Force plane returning to the United States from Churchill's funeral. They had once been close friends but Harriman had become a bitter critic when Ike ran for president as a Republican. Eisenhower and Harry Truman had their first real conversation in more than a decade at JFK's funeral. While their friendship would never be repaired, their enmity and rancor softened for the moment. But sometimes such occasions demanded too much from Eisenhower. He could not bring himself to attend the funeral of his former boss, General Douglas MacArthur.

Like other former presidents, Eisenhower was aiming for the history books. He arranged for the publication of his letters and private papers by the Johns Hopkins University Press. He wrote two volumes of White House memoirs; and he gave scores of interviews to scholars and historians. Eisenhower, with confidence in his leadership and his judgments, believed that he would be well treated by future generations of historians.

It rankled him, though, that some members of the academic elite sneered at his administration and poked fun at him. Soon after leaving the White House, Ike suffered something of an embarrassment when the *New York Times Magazine* featured a poll of scholars that ranked him among the nation's ten worst chief executives. Eisenhower, a skillful poker player, had fallen victim to a stacked deck. Arthur M. Schlesinger, Sr., who took the survey, had been a prominent supporter of Eisenhower's erstwhile Democratic opponent, Governor Adlai E. Stevenson. Other participants in the survey included two of Stevenson's speechwriters, a leader in the 1952 "Draft Stevenson" movement, and other Democratic activists. So it was not that much of surprise that a group ranked Eisenhower between White House mediocrities Chester Alan Arthur and Andrew Johnson. It was said that John F. Kennedy got a big laugh out of Eisenhower's low score in the survey.

Eisenhower's critics were chortling even more in 1963 when a former speechwriter, Emmet John Hughes, published a kiss-and-tell book about Ike's presidency entitled *The Ordeal of Power*. In the book, Hughes reinforced the Herblock cartoon stereotypes of Eisenhower as an amiable bumbler, bored with matters of substance. Hughes portrayed Eisenhower as weak and indecisive in the mold of James Buchanan. The second Eisenhower term was portrayed as a series of hapless fumbles and mischances.

Eisenhower broke with his tradition of not commenting about books by former aides in a background interview with journalist Robert T. Hartmann. He believed that Hughes had violated the confidences of private conversations and that the former speechwriter had falsified Ike's comments about John Foster Dulles to get back at Dulles for having prevented Hughes from gaining an appointment to a senior position in the State Department. But even before the publication of this book, Hughes had fallen from favor with Eisenhower. And when New York Governor Nelson A. Rockefeller named Hughes as his speechwriter and political adviser, he, too, paid a price. Although Rockefeller had been Ike's national security adviser, Eisenhower froze him out in the 1960s for giving the acerbic Hughes a new political base. Without Eisenhower's blessing, Rockefeller had great difficulty claiming the mantle of Eisenhower's modern Republicanism.

Ike's political coattails, which got shorter in each succeeding election during his presidency, were threadbare in his retirement. He campaigned for James Mitchell, his former labor secretary, Who ran for governor of New Jersey; for Fred

Seaton, his former interior secretary, in his bid for governor of Nebraska; and for Nixon, his former vice president, who later ran for governor of California. Eisenhower had won all three states in both of his presidential campaigns, but his popularity was not transferable. Mitchell, Seaton, and Nixon were all defeated in their political comebacks.

In his adopted state of Pennsylvania, Eisenhower had significantly more political influence than in the states where he barnstormed for former cabinet members. From his Gettysburg farm, Eisenhower became the dominant force in the Pennsylvania Republican party and the architect for its return to power in Harrisburg. When Pennsylvania's Old Guard Republican bosses attempted to nominate an undistinguished judge, Robert E. Woodside, as their candidate for the governorship, Eisenhower told Senator Hugh Scott that Woodside would be a "miserable" choice. Ike tried and failed to persuade his former Defense Secretary Thomas Gates and former State Department official William W. Scranton, then a freshman congressman, to make the race. When they declined, Eisenhower lobbied Scott to run. Through some deft maneuvering, Scott persuaded the state's GOP leadership to make a conditional endorsement of Scranton. And it was Eisenhower who persuaded Scranton to run for governor. With Ike's strong support in the fall campaign, Scranton became the first GOP governor in eight years.

Having a similar impact nationally was much more difficult. In the early 1960s he organized the Republican Citizens Committee as the successor to Citizens for Eisenhower. But without his presidential candidacy, the Republican Citizens Committee was nothing more than a letterhead with some big names printed on its border. Eisenhower had private misgivings about Democratic presidents Kennedy and Johnson, but he thought it would be counterproductive to publicly attack them. By training and temperament,

Eisenhower was of the old school that supported presidential leadership in foreign policy. In contrast to the dissenting voices of Herbert Hoover in the 1930s and Jimmy Carter in the 1980s, Eisenhower shunned the role of critic in world affairs. Just as he had supported the foreign policies of Roosevelt and Truman in the 1940s, Eisenhower endorsed the foreign policies of Kennedy and Johnson in the 1960s, including their escalation of the Vietnam War—even though that was a reversal of his own policy of restraint.

Another reason the Republican Citizens fizzled was that the Republican party's established institutions, the Republican National Committee and the Republican congressional leadership, were much more forceful in their criticism of the national Democratic administration. Goldwater emerged as the leader of the first genuine political revolution since Huey Long's populist crusade of the Great Depression. Eisenhower was uncomfortable with populist movements and sought to help the Republican establishment thwart the right-wing revolt.

His first choice for the 1964 Republican presidential nomination was his youngest brother, Milton Eisenhower. But Milton, who had declined opportunities to run for the U.S. Senate and the governorship of Maryland, was not interested. Neither were the others on Ike's short list: former Treasury Secretary Robert B. Anderson, and Generals Alfred Gruenther and Lucius Clay. In November 1963, Eisenhower had urged Henry Cabot Lodge, then serving as U.S. ambassador to South Vietnam, to return and seek the presidency. Lodge, though, demurred after JFK's assassination. Eisenhower was not enthused about either of the leading Republican contenders—Goldwater or Rockefeller.

Neither, it turned out, were most Republican voters. In March 1964, Lodge scored a dramatic write-in victory over the front-runners in the New Hampshire primary with the help of a media blitz that featured an old film clip of Eisenhower praising Lodge. For a brief time, it appeared as if Lodge might seriously challenge the active contenders. But his hopes were dimmed when Rockefeller edged him out in the Oregon primary. Shortly before the California primary, Eisenhower published a front-page statement in the *New York Herald Tribune* in which he appeared to be calling for Goldwater's rejection in the primaries. Eisenhower, however, promptly backed off when his former Treasury secretary, George Humphrey, urged him not to get involved in a bitter power struggle between Goldwater and Rockefeller.

Ike's neutrality worked to Goldwater's advantage. The Arizona senator narrowly won the California primary over Rockefeller and was closing in on the nomination. Eisenhower, who viewed Goldwater as a loose cannon, was troubled by the prospect of his nomination. The former president encouraged Scranton to launch a late-starting bid for the Republican nomination. Neither Eisenhower nor Scranton looked strong or decisive in their attempt to stop Goldwater. The reluctant Scranton held back when Eisenhower stopped short of an endorsement.

Eisenhower turned up the heat on Scranton after Goldwater voted against the 1964 Civil Rights Bill. The former president told Scranton that it was his duty to run for the nomination to defend the legacy of Lincoln. But when Scranton plunged into the 1964 campaign, Eisenhower's testimonial was lacking the only words that counted. Without a specific reference to Scranton, Eisenhower said that the San Francisco convention should nominate a Republican for the presidency who favored equality for blacks. In the end, Scranton got more help from other members of the Eisenhower family. Milton Eisenhower placed Scranton's name in nomination; and Ike's son, John, worked for Scranton during the convention. Concluding that he should not indulge in partisan controversies, Eisenhower declined to endorse Scranton or to speak out in favor of Scranton's platform minority planks on limiting the use of nuclear weapons and strengthening civil rights laws. It was not Eisenhower's finest hour.

In what would be his farewell appearance at a Republican national convention, Eisenhower touched off an explosion of cheers with his rip-snorting attacks on permissive judges and "sensation-seeking" columnists. But it was not his convention, and he knew it. More than a few of the right-wing faithful in the Cow Palace in San Francisco had distributed John Birch Society literature in which Eisenhower had been depicted, along with FDR and General George Marshall, as a Soviet dupe. Eisenhower was appalled by Goldwater's acceptance speech in which he defended political extremism and denounced moderation. In a real sense, the Goldwater nomination was a rejection of Eisenhower's brand of Republicanism.

Even so, Eisenhower supported Goldwater but with minimal enthusiasm. He was not surprised that Goldwater was buried in an electoral avalanche. Eisenhower had privately observed that Goldwater was not electable because of the perception that he was aligned with the lunatic fringe.

While some respected commentators were writing obituaries for the Republican party in the wake of its worst defeat in three decades, Eisenhower renewed his efforts to promote new leadership. He was among the first prominent Republicans to urge the election of a new national chairman, setting the stage for the elevation of Ray Bliss of Ohio to the party's leadership. In 1965, Eisenhower hosted four hundred prominent Republicans at his Gettysburg farm for discussions about their party's future. By the primaries of 1968, his health was failing and he could no longer play an active role. His endorsement of Nixon just before the Miami convention gave Nixon a burst of momentum; and it reminded Rockefeller, the other major contender, that Eisenhower had not forgiven him for having Hughes among his senior advisers.

It would be a rarity for a former president of the United States to have major influence in the shaping of national policy beyond his term of office; and Eisenhower was no exception to the rule. Because of his extraordinary and enduring popularity, Eisenhower was consulted by Presidents Kennedy, Johnson, and Nixon. While they cultivated relationships with Eisenhower, it was for their political benefit. None of Ike's successors wanted to risk alienating a former president who was still the most popular man in America. Each of them listened politely to Eisenhower's advice and later quietly ignored it. Eisenhower was viewed, like Dean Acheson and Harry Truman, as more of a historical figure than a political player in the 1960s.

In his retirement, Eisenhower managed to make a strong case for his place in history. He had once confided, "I think I pretty well hit my peak in history when I accepted the German surrender." But there were growing signs in the last five years of Eisenhower's life that he would ultimately gain recognition as one of the nation's better chief executives.

Eisenhower's own two-volume history of his presidency was more authoritative but less provocative than those written by his critics, and the books had little immediate impact on his reputation. His refusal to disclose his unvarnished opinion of political contemporaries or to admit mistakes was in keeping with the bland tone that he set for both volumes.

In the first volume of his memoirs, without revealing the other man's identity, Eisenhower described a secret meeting with a prominent Republican senator at the Pentagon in the winter of 1951. At the meeting, Eisenhower offered to renounce all political ambitions if the senator would make a public commitment to economic and military aid to Western Europe and participation in the North Atlantic Treaty Organization. When the senator declined, Eisenhower began thinking much more seriously about running for the presidency.

The meeting had been a turning point in modern American history because the senator Eisenhower neglected to identify in his book was Robert A. Taft, the leading contender at the time for the 1952 Republican presidential nomination. Ike's memoirs would have been much more compelling reading if he had written what he had told associates—that as a result of their meeting, he considered Taft a very stupid man. Had the Ohio senator accepted Eisenhower's offer at the Pentagon, it is more than likely that he would have been nominated for the presidency and Eisenhower would have remained in uniform.

There was much solid, first-hand information, though, in Eisenhower's memoirs for future scholars of his presidency. Murray Kempton, drawing from Ike's memoirs and from his own background as one of the era's more prominent journalists, wrote the first influential revisionist interpretation, "The Underestimation of Dwight D. Eisenhower," for *Esquire* in September 1967. "He is revealed best, if only occasionally, in the vast and dreary acreage of his memoirs of the White House years," wrote Kempton. "The Eisenhower who emerges here . . . is the president most superbly equipped for truly consequential decisions we may ever have had, a mind neither rash nor hesitant, free of the slightest concern for how things might look, indifferent to any sentiment, as calm when he was demonstrating the wisdom of leaving a bad situation alone as when he was moving to meet it on those occasions when he absolutely had to."

Eisenhower never doubted that he would be well remembered. By making public his private correspondence, presidential papers, and diaries, most of which were not opened until after his death in 1969, Eisenhower made the largest contribution to the rehabilitation of his historical image. A poll of scholars taken in 1982 ranked him among the ten best presidents and his reputation is continuing to improve. In the final months of his presidency, Eisenhower made this private assessment of his style: "In war and peace I've had no respect for the desk-pounder, and have despised the loud and slick talker. If my own ideas and practices in this matter have sprung from weakness, I do not know. But they were and are deliberate or, rather, natural to me. They are not accidental."

Nor, it turns out, is the revisionist assessment of his administration. As a keen student of history, Eisenhower made better use of his ex-presidency than most of his predecessors. More than a few of his skeptics have now acknowledged that the American voter was right to like Ike. And had it not been for the Twenty-second Amendment, they would have extended his lease on the White House for as long as he wanted.

Former President Lyndon B. Johnson at the Hoover Library.

V

TWILIGHT
ON THE
PEDERNALES

"All I could accomplish would be to make a fool of myself," LBJ replied [to a question about his participation in the 1972 Democratic campaign]. "I don't hold public office. I don't have a party position. I don't have a platform. I don't have any troops." And then he winked at me and, with typical Lyndon Johnson understatement, said: "The only thing more impotent than a former president is a cut dog at a screwing match."

I think my own comprehension of Johnson is that he continued to grow in the White House, at least expand his vision; and he continued to grow in his retirement. The final speech that he made at the civil rights symposium a month before his death took him further along the line of what he felt the nation should do to redress ancient injustice than he had gone even in the White House.

—Robert L. Hardesty

—Harry J. Middleton

With Lyndon Johnson in Texas:
A Memoir of
the Post-Presidential Years

ROBERT L. HARDESTY

I wrote a column for *Newsweek* magazine a number of years ago in which I called our former presidents, "a squandered national resource." I pointed out that one minute they are standing at the pinnacle of power where they learn to deal with prime ministers, presidents, monarchs, dictators, and petty tyrants; where they lead the nation along the perilous razor's edge between security and holocaust; where they learn to judge the pulse of human needs and human aspirations; where they develop a grasp of international affairs that few men or women ever possess—and then we dump them unceremoniously on the rubbish heap of history. In a single day's time, we turn our backs on a lifetime of training and knowledge and experience and public esteem and political know-how.

Lyndon Johnson was certainly no exception. He had been in public office almost all of his adult life—congressman, senator, majority leader, vice president, and president. He had been a supreme activist, a human whirlwind. He had used the power of office to bring about change. Reform was central to his philosophy. The status quo was an abomination to his very being.

Power was his oxygen—and he breathed it deeply. Then suddenly it was gone, and not in the happiest of circumstances. "I know we're leaving office pretty well repudiated," he told us in the closing months of the presidency.

There is no doubt in my mind that he would have liked to have had another four years in office to further solidify the gains of his Great Society programs, especially in the areas of health care, education, and civil rights. Despite his own concerns about his health, I do not think he was ready to go. He repeatedly told his audiences the story of the delegation of temperance ladies who came to visit Winston Churchill in the height of World War II. They came to complain about the prime minister's drinking habits. "Mr. Prime Minister," one of the ladies said, "if all the brandy that you drank in a year was poured into this room, it would come halfway up to the ceiling." And she held up her hand to dramatize the point. The prime minister looked solemnly at the floor. Then he looked at the ceiling. Then he looked at the lady's hand at the midmark. And he muttered very sadly, "So little done. So much yet to do."

It always got a laugh, but it was a rueful tale. So much yet to do. But Johnson thought that maybe, just maybe, if he took himself out of the running—out of politics—he could get the North Vietnamese to negotiate a settlement to that dreadful, tragic, interminable war in Southeast Asia.

Peace with honor—his whole being yearned for it, ached for it. But it was not to come, not during his term of office—indeed, not during his lifetime. So there he was as his term drew to a close: frustrated in his hopes for peace, "repudiated," his ability to govern severely impaired, and his domestic agenda uncompleted.

Those of us who went from the White House to Texas with him—Harry Middleton, Tom Johnson, Walt Rostow, Bill Jorden and I—were prepared for the worst. He would be, we were warned, impossible to live with. He would be like a caged tiger with all that pent-up energy, alternately roaring at those around him, out of frustration, and then sulking in a corner out of self-pity.

Indeed, that is what most of the press expected too, and, with them, it became a self-fulfilling prophecy. They could not imagine him any other way, so that is the way they depicted him during most of the years of his retirement: a sullen, bitter, brooding, unhappy man, retreating to the isolation of his ranch to lick his wounds.

But the press never could predict Lyndon Johnson and that is not the way it happened. Part of the misconception stemmed from the fact that the press did not see much of him. The truth was he simply had no desire to have reporters around him. "I'm not in that business any more," he often said. "I'm a private citizen now."

Someone made a needlepoint pillow for him shortly before his retirement. It bore the motto: "This is my ranch and I do as I damn well please." That pillow occupied a prominent place of honor on the living room sofa. It seemed to sum up his entire philosophy of retirement.

He was tired, God knows, bone tired and he needed some time to recharge his batteries. He did retreat to the ranch, but not to sulk. He threw himself headlong into the only hobby he had ever known: ranching. He had always gone back to the land to draw his strength and to renew his perspective. The only difference now was that he was doing it full time. And there was only one person around him who had reason to wish that he was back in the White House: his ranch foreman, Dale Malachek.

So completely did he throw himself into ranching that it was difficult to get him to focus on the business at hand. And for those of us on his staff, the business at hand was the drafting of his memoirs, *The Vantage Point*. A chapter conference could be a very frustrating experience. Imagine sitting in an open Lincoln convertible with an archives box of presidential papers in your lap, bouncing around the rugged terrain of the Texas hill country, the wind blowing documents all over the car. Imagine trying to get a former president of the United States to focus on an obscure historical incident while he was driving all over the ranch, incessantly barking orders at his foreman over the radio and stopping when the mood struck him to help the ranch hands move huge segments of irrigation pipe from one pasture to another. Some chapter conference!

It soon became clear to me that he just was not ready yet to begin focusing on the memoirs. So I solved that problem—for myself at least—by having a massive coronary and going out of circulation for three months. When I returned, he was ready to go to work.

Gradually, however, a pattern in his activities began to emerge. It became clear that he was indulging himself in the one thing he never had enough of during his career: leisure time. He now had time for his family, time for his friends, time for pet projects, time for travel. He even found time for an occasional game of golf. Instead of chaffing at the unaccustomed experience of having time on his hands, he reveled in it and he used it.

The guest rooms at the ranch were always full. The guests came in an endless flow: old staffers, old colleagues, old friends—politicians, industrialists, moguls, movie stars. The agenda seldom changed. There were always late-afternoon tours of the ranch in a caravan of cars and station wagons: showing off the exotic game, feeding a pet deer, and drinking several long, cool scotch and sodas at the highest point of the ranch while watching the blazing Texas sun sink slowly into the west. Afterward, there would be a long, leisurely dinner with lots of teasing and good conversation. If the guest was rich enough, he or she was usually persuaded to leave a hefty check behind to help finance the activities of the Johnson Library and the Johnson School of Public Affairs.

Central to LBJ's happiness, to his contentment, to his

peace of mind, and to his very being was his beloved wife, Lady Bird. She understood him as no other person on earth. She mellowed him. She softened him. She slowed him down. She placated him. She tempered his rashness with a sense of calm, penetrating judgment that he had long since come to depend on. It would be too much to say that without Lady Bird Johnson there would have been no Lyndon Johnson—but it would have been a far different Lyndon Johnson than the one we came to know.

I saw the Johnsons operate together as a couple on a regular and, indeed, sometimes daily basis after they left the White House and returned to Texas. I became more and more impressed with Lady Bird's resiliency, her generous use of private time, her positive approach to every situation, her quiet self-confidence that gave her the strength to meet any challenge head on, no matter how daunting it might look to others. Her favorite response to those who would sometimes become dismayed and exasperated by the demands LBJ made on other people, including, I might add, my own wife, was: "My dear, just look on it all as one great adventure." Indeed, I think that sums up Lady Bird Johnson's philosophy of life as well as any one sentence can.

But as central as she was to her husband's daily life, and as much as she gave herself to it, she never lost her own identity. She continued to take part in all of his games and plans without losing her firm sense of self. She had always maintained some kind of agenda of her own, even in the face of the strong-willed whirlwind she had married, and she began in her husband's retirement years to further develop the interests and lay the foundation for what would become the central public and professional focus of her later widowhood: the National Wildflower Research Center, which she established and endowed and to which she continues to give the bulk of her time and support.

Lady Bird Johnson is one of those people who wears well the better you get to know her. The more trying the circumstances under which I saw her and the more closely I observed her reaction, the more I came to admire her. Each layer of her personality revealed another remarkable facet, another deep strength on which she drew and on which those around her have come to rely. She is truly a remarkable lady and she always brought out the best in Lyndon Johnson.

In the four years of his retirement, LBJ's physical appearance changed dramatically. His face and hands became deeply tanned and weathered from constant exposure to the Texas sun, and his hair begun to turn white. Always conscious of fashion, he shed himself of the dark suits and ties of his Washington days and began to dress in the "mod" fashion of the early 1970s—bold, striped shirts; wide, bright ties; and colorful sport coats.

Even I had an influence on his appearance. We were sitting on the lawn in front of the ranch house one morning, discussing the memoirs. It was the first time I had been to the ranch since my heart attack and I had not had a haircut during my entire three-month convalescence. Predictably, the president commented on it. "Robert, your hair is getting a little long, isn't it?" One of my lifelong downfalls is that if I do not have a reasonable answer, I tend to give a smart-assed one. So I replied, "Yes, Mr. President, that's so I won't look like that short-haired crowd in the Nixon White House."

He peered at me suspiciously through those narrowed eyes. "Short-haired crowd?" "Sure: Erlichman, Haldeman, Ziegler, the whole bunch." He abruptly changed the subject as if he could not deal with such an idiotic conversation and I immediately wished I had just told him I had not had time to get a haircut. But the next time I saw him, several weeks later, his hair was creeping down over his shirt collar, and within a couple of months, he was beginning to look from the rear like a tall William Jennings Bryan; even the press was commenting on it.

As LBJ's energy increased, so did his activities. The progress of his Great Society programs was a matter of continuing interest to him, and if he could no longer direct those programs on a national scale, it did not prevent him from doing so locally. So he started a Headstart class for poor Mexican-American children in Stonewall, near the ranch, and even volunteered to do some of the car-pooling. He was known to those children, not as "Mr. President" or as "Mr. Johnson" but as "Mr. Jelly Bean" because of the prodigious amounts of candy he handed out on his regular visits to the school.

Gradually, even the LBJ Ranch could not use up all of his energy, so he rented another ranch—a larger one—in Mexico. And there, he started another Headstart program for poor Mexican children and personally saw to it that they received a good, hot meal every day and regular physical checkups and eye exams.

Every winter there was a month-long retreat to former Mexican President Valdes Aleman's sprawling, multilevel house in Alcapulco, with its own private beach. It really was not a change of pace so much as it was a change of venue. The guests came and went as usual. Each was properly outfitted for the Mexican tropics upon arrival: long, colorful native dresses for the women and white trousers and loose guayabera shirts for the men.

My wife, Mary, remembered those Alcapulco vacations in an article she wrote shortly after LBJ's death: "President and Mrs. Johnson spent every February in a lovely sprawling hacienda with a breathtaking view of a mountain-ringed bay, vermillion sunsets, and tropical jungle foliage. Anyone but Johnson would have gone quietly and thanked God for the rest. He, instead, took a large portion of Texas with him, both mechanical and human, and imported people from east and west to help him fill the days.

"Meals were wonderful, long ceremonies in the French manner, a stage for Johnson to show his natural acting ability as a comedian and mimic. With perfect timing, he told stories of his own personal past, political memories, jokes— and commentaries on current national and global events and the people making it all happen. His mind was sharp, enthusiastic and generally optimistic."

Of course, wherever he was, part of his days were spent tending to his far-flung business interests—in broadcasting, banking, and land. He owned, I believe, very little stock. He had a populist's ingrained distrust of the stock market and he once berated my wife rather severely when he learned that she, a self-proclaimed liberal Democrat, owned some utility stock. He brushed off the explanation that she had inherited the stock from her father; the memories of LBJ's heated battles in the 1930s to bring cheap electricity to poor rural Texas were too fresh in his mind to accept any explanation.

There was one ongoing activity that spanned almost the entire four years of his retirement: the filming of his interviews with Walter Cronkite for CBS. Eventually, they completed seven one-hour shows: on the space program, on the president's decision not to seek reelection in 1968, on the decision to halt the bombing in Vietnam, on the Kennedy assassination and the days of transition, on Harry Truman, on politics, and on civil rights.

These were intense sessions—before, during, and afterward—and not always amicable. Throughout his career, LBJ prepared himself thoroughly for everything he did, whether it was a Senate debate, an interview, a press conference, or a meeting. He left nothing to chance. And so, days before each filming, the staff would shuttle back and forth between Austin and the ranch with boxes of documents for the former president to study and discuss. Each document set off a search for three more and by the time filming was to begin, everyone was exhausted except the president.

There was a certain amount of tension between President Johnson and Walter Cronkite. They had been old friends, but Cronkite had split with LBJ over the war in Vietnam and things were never quite the same after that. During the filming, Cronkite and producer Bud Benjamin took their meals with the Johnsons and there was always an air of relaxed conviviality around the table, but the tension persisted. Not that LBJ wanted anybody but Cronkite to do the interviews. Cronkite was the best in the business and he was a supreme professional—qualities that Johnson admired almost above all others.

But the real problems came after the filming, when we got a chance to see the working script of how CBS was planning to put the show together. Naturally, CBS could not use the entire interview, so they had to cut and splice. It was the way they cut and spliced that sometimes led to trouble. In several instances, they used a Johnson answer to an entirely different Cronkite question and it changed the meaning of the answer entirely. This was particularly troublesome when they were dealing with sensitive issues like Vietnam. On those occasions, there would be an explosion at the ranch. Staff would be summoned. Phone calls would be made to New York. Law suits were threatened. Sometimes the producer would backdown. Sometimes he would not. When he would not, lawyers would be summoned. More phone calls would be made. Eventually a compromise would be reached. Tempers would cool down. And by the time the crew showed up at the ranch, months later, for the next interview, it was as though nothing had ever happened.

Unfortunately, the memoirs—*The Vantage Point*—did not have such a happy ending. They were accurate, interesting, truthful, and historically significant—but totally lacking in color; totally lacking in LBJ. Somewhere in the process, LBJ the humorist, LBJ the storyteller, LBJ the mimic, LBJ the raconteur got completely lost. Those of us who were working on the book would sit down with him to discuss a particular chapter in its early stages and religiously take down his comments and observations and weave them into the chapter. One example comes immediately to mind. He was dealing with the Gulf of Tonkin Resolution and Senator William Fulbright's subsequent assertion that he would not have voted for it if he had known what kind of powers it gave the president. LBJ commented: "For a Rhodes Scholar to say he didn't know what that resolution said is more than this hillbilly is prepared to believe."

Well, once a chapter had been written and gone over by him and honed and edited and rewritten, the sanitation process began. He would send it to half a dozen trusted friends and informal advisers around the country who promptly cut out all the color. "It doesn't sound presidential," they told him, whatever that meant. Can you imagine how Harry Truman would appear in history if his advisers had told *him* that? Or Andy Jackson? Or Abe Lincoln? The writers protested, of course, but we always lost. The offensive comment or passage was deleted.

The same thing happened to his harsh or derisive comments about some of the individuals who loomed large in his years. In person, LBJ could have you in stitches when he ridiculed some pompous ass. But every time the writers captured it, the advisers would veto it. "You don't want to needlessly offend people, Mr. President," they would say. So in the end, we had a book about the Johnson administration that contained very little of Johnson the *man*. And that's a great pity to those of us who really knew him.

LBJ's most important activities in retirement were directed toward his final consuming passion: the LBJ Library and the LBJ School of Public Affairs in Austin. All of the money that he made from his book, his CBS interviews, and his speeches and lectures went into a special foundation whose sole purpose was to support the library and school. Although these contributions ran into the millions, he could easily have doubled that if he had accepted all of the speaking engagements that he received. But as it was, he accepted very few. He did not want to appear to be forcing himself on an unwilling public.

If LBJ was hurt and morose over the nation's "repudiation" of him—and he was—he was also a realist. He kept a low profile because he was convinced—rightly I believe—that most people were not particularly interested in what he had to say. "I've had my day," he would explain. "I've spoken my piece. Other people occupy that stage now."

He was particularly resistant to efforts to get him involved in Democratic party politics. Although he was happy to speak on behalf of a public official who had been a close friend and ally of his, he adamantly rejected the role of "kingmaker." He believed strongly that Harry Truman had made a major mistake—and had hurt himself in the process—by actively promoting the presidential candidacy of New York Governor Averell Harriman at the 1956 Democratic convention.

No one was beating his door down for his public support as the 1972 Democratic convention neared, but there were many who would have welcomed his behind-the-scenes assistance. He still had friends and many of them were party regulars, but he simply refused to get involved. Late in 1971, in my presence, he told CBS producer Bud Benjamin why. Benjamin asked him if he was going to get involved in the upcoming Democratic presidential campaign.

"No," the president answered immediately and firmly, "in no way." Benjamin expressed surprise. "I would have thought you'd respond to a political campaign like an old fire horse, after all the ones you've been through." "All I could accomplish would be to make a fool of myself," LBJ replied. "I don't hold public office. I don't have a party position. I don't have a platform. I don't have any troops." And then he winked at me and, with typical Lyndon Johnson understatement, said to Benjamin: "The only thing more impotent than a former president is a cut dog at a screwing match."

Toward the end, however, Johnson did speak out more, but in a positive way, and on issues that had been central to the Great Society. He was adamant in his refusal to make life difficult for President Nixon by criticizing him or second-guessing him. He had a stage from which to speak now—the LBJ Library—and he began to use it. The library was completed in 1971 and in the spring of 1972, there was a huge dedication and subsequent reunion of virtually all of the Great Society veterans. It was to be his "last hurrah" with his appointees and friends and staff—the last big gathering of the clan during his lifetime.

After the library opened, its director, Harry Middleton, began planning a series of symposia on major issues of the day and two of these were held before LBJ's death: one on education and the other on civil rights—the cornerstones of the Great Society. When it came to these issues, Johnson had lost none of the fire in his belly. He believed, as he said many times, that education is the only valid passport out of poverty and that civil rights was the moral imperative of his generation.

The end was in sight now—Johnson had suffered two

heart attacks since returning to Texas and he was constantly popping nitroglycerine tablets to quell the angina pains. Yet he would not slow down; he wanted to use all the time he had left to help keep the nation on course.

At the education symposium he told the speakers, panelists, and guests that they were not there to celebrate the breakthroughs of yesterday but to try to chart the breakthroughs of tomorrow. "I have never had as high an opinion of the past as I have of the future," he said—and what a typical Johnson statement that was. And then, as if he were looking sixteen years into the future, to a time when education is again at the forefront of America's agenda, he made this declaration: "This country has the money to do anything it has the guts to do, and the vision to do and the will to do." I think he would still hold to that belief today.

The civil rights symposium took place just six weeks before President Johnson's death. His health was so precarious that his doctor told him he could not attend. The doctor might just as well have saved his breath. With some of the true giants of the civil rights movement in attendance—Earl Warren, Vernon Jordan, Hubert Humphrey, Roy Wilkins, Clarence Mitchell, Julian Bond, Barbara Jordan, and Burke Marshall—LBJ would have arrived on a stretcher, had it been necessary. These were his people, the men and women who had toiled with him in the vineyards of American justice for nearly twenty years.

He closed that conference with one of the most eloquent pleas for affirmative action he had ever made, declaring that, "to be black in a white society is not to stand on level and equal ground. While the races may stand side by side, whites stand on history's mountain and blacks stand in history's hollow. We must overcome unequal history," he insisted, "before we overcome unequal opportunity."

Afterward, in response to an unexpected attack on President Nixon from the audience, he returned to the podium, slowly now, his breath labored, angina pains gripping his chest. He was there to make his last plea for reason over bitterness and confrontation. He urged the civil rights leaders to counsel with the president, not to threaten him. A president *wants* to do right, he said. "He doesn't want to leave the presidency feeling that he's been unfair or unjust to his fellow man."

"I served with many presidents," he said, "and I think I have a viewpoint that no other person in this room has about the presidency." And then, as he had done so often in his career, he illustrated his point with a story: "Out in my little town, Court Week is very exciting," he said. "All the boys leave town to avoid the grand jury and all the citizens go to court to hear the proceedings. The town drunk, hung over, came up to the hotel one morning as the old judge was leaving and said, 'Would you give a poor man a dime for a cup of coffee?' And the judge said, 'Hell, no; get out of the way. I wouldn't give a tramp anything.' The poor fellow with the hangover walked off dejectedly, and just as he got to the end of the porch, the judge said, 'Come back. If you'd like to have a quarter for a pick-me-up, I'd be glad to help you.' And he handed the old fellow a quarter. The drunk looked up at him startled, but with great appreciation in his eyes and said, 'Judge, you've been there, haven't you.'"

That was not the last time I saw Lyndon Johnson, but that is the way I will always remember him: with a story and an object lesson and the ability to laugh in the face of death.

A President and His Library:
My Recollections of Working with Lyndon B. Johson

HARRY J. MIDDLETON

I would like to concentrate on Lyndon Johnson's involvement with his presidential library because I think it provides a unique perspective on his activities as a former president. To set the stage, I must explain how I became the director of the LBJ Library.

I was neither an archivist nor a historian when I was appointed director. Before working for Johnson in the White House, I had been a journalist. In short, I had absolutely no qualifications to be director of a presidential library except for the fact that I had worked for President Johnson and he believed that the people who worked for him were generalists and could do anything. So I was really quite lucky that he did not see to it that I was appointed foreman of his ranch!

I was involved in those very early months after my appointment in an extensive on-the-job training program, learning what presidential libraries were supposed to do, what they were all about, what directors of presidential libraries did to earn their pay. That is the background.

The library's first major project about a year after its dedication was to open the papers relating to education and to commemorate the event with a symposium at which the leaders in the field would discuss further initiatives that the government might take. Johnson was intensely interested in the symposium. I met with him at the ranch frequently and talked with him almost daily on the phone about the plans.

In the meantime, the archivists were reviewing the papers. The questions of whether to open certain sensitive materials came to me for resolution. Since I was new to the experience and unsure of myself, most of these problems stayed on my desk in a state of limbo.

About ten days before the symposium, Johnson called and this time he wanted to talk about the papers. "We're opening everything that has anything to do with education, aren't we?" he asked. "Well, all that can be opened," I answered. "Now what does that mean?" he demanded. I reminded him of the deed of gift that he had signed when he turned the papers over to the government. Following usual procedure, the deed stipulated that papers injurious or embarrassing to living persons should be kept closed for a while.

He pretended not to understand what I was saying, a typical Johnson ploy. "Give me an example," he said. I had a desktop full of such examples, and I picked one. It was a memorandum from Joe Califano to the president with a rather scurrilous reference to Congresswoman Edith Green. After I read it to LBJ, there was a silence. Then Johnson said, "Edith's heard worse things than that. Who else is that memo going to hurt?" I pointed out that Califano, then Democratic party counsel, was working with a lot of people from different camps and might be troubled by it. "When you were appointed director of the library," Johnson said, "was there anything in your job description that said you were supposed to try to hold the Democratic party together?"

He asked for other examples, and I gave him several. He disposed of all of them in much the same fashion. Then he said, "Are you going to try and treat me the same way?" Choosing my way carefully, I said that he deserved the same consideration anyone else did, but he interrupted. "Good men have been trying to save my reputation for forty years," he said, "and not a damn one succeeded. What makes you think you can?"

Another silence and then, "I suppose you think that if I pick up the paper one day and read something in these files that I don't like, I'll raise hell." "Mr. President," I acknowledged, "that thought has occurred to me." "Well if that ever happens," he said, "here's what I want you to do: I want you to go out and sit on the hill in front of the library and take a lot of deep breaths and think of everything we've been through to get this library opened, and then you come back to your office and you call me. I'll be right here waiting for your call because I'll be expecting it. You say, 'Mr. President' because that's the way you talk, you're always very polite, 'Mr. President, one of us is full of shit and we've got to decide right now who it is.'"

So one of the things that LBJ did in his retirement, in those four years of his ex-presidency, was to set the policy that the library has followed in regard to access to archival materials. It has been, I think, a liberal policy.

Johnson also was responsible in large part for the symposia. I had been director of the library for the year preceding its dedication and all of our attentions were focused on getting the library opened and ready for dedication. On a Sunday afternoon exactly one week after the library was dedicated, my wife came into the room where I had the Sunday papers all spread out and she said, "My God, President and Mrs. Johnson are at the door." Our house is right across the street from an Episcopal church in Austin. It turned out that the Johnsons were supposed to go to a ceremony at that church but Mrs. Johnson had misread the invitation and they had gotten there an hour early. President Johnson knew a place where he could sit down, so they came over to our place.

In situations like that, he was never much for small talk.

When he got in, he said, "We've opened that library and dedicated it. Now what are we going to do?" I had just a glimmer of an idea. It was not anything that I wanted to talk about. I was not prepared to, but there was no way out of it. I said that I had an idea that I had been toying with; we ought to select the first group of papers to open for research with a subject that was close to him and I thought education would be a good idea. Perhaps as we did that, I said, we could have a conference of leaders of the field to discuss initiatives that the government might take in the future.

The words were hardly out of my mouth when he put the LBJ stamp on it. "We'll do that," he said, "let's do that. Then right after that we'll open the civil rights papers and we'll have a conference on civil rights. Now, we're here on this university campus. We can't do it all by ourselves. The university has the brain power, our foundation has some money. Take Lady Bird with you tomorrow morning, and go over and see the president of the university and tell him what we want to do. See if he'll set up a committee." He had the whole thing outlined.

The next morning, I did call the president of the university and told him that LBJ had asked me to come over and see him in the company of Mrs. Johnson and he agreed to make the time available. So I collected Mrs. Johnson and she was rather bewildered. On the way over she said, "What is it we're going to talk about?" I was not entirely sure myself, but we saw Steve Spurr, who was then the new president of the university, told him about the conversation and he immediately appointed a committee. This committee included Bob Hardesty as a member of President Johnson's staff, me as a representative of the library, and about eight of the leading lights of the university campus. This group became the planning committee for a series of substantive conferences that have continued to this day. These conferences are really the legacy of Lyndon Johnson, a contribution that he made in the years of his ex-presidency.

I think my own comprehension of Johnson is that he continued to grow in the White House, at least expand his vision; and he continued to grow in his retirement. The final speech that he made at the civil rights symposium a month before his death took him further along the line of what he felt the nation should do to redress ancient injustice than he had gone even in the White House.

Toward the end of his life, he did not talk about death much, but it was on his mind. I remember that he attended the memorial service of a friend held in a Catholic cathedral. Although he had shown a decided interest in Catholicism, this interest did not extend to ceremonial pomp. The air in the cathedral was close and stuffy, the odor of incense cloying, and the mourners were the celebrated figures of the day. The service prompted him to make sure his own wishes were clear.

"When I die," he told Lady Bird in the company of a few guests, "I don't just want our friends who can come in their private planes. I want the men in their pick-up trucks and the women whose slips hang down below their dresses to be welcome too." When he was buried in the family graveyard along the Pedernales River on a cold January afternoon ten days later, they were all there: the men who landed their planes on the runway, and the neighbors from the ranches in towns around who brought their families by truck.

Before he was buried, his body lay in the library in Austin and in the rotunda of the Capitol in Washington. Lady Bird and their daughters with their husbands stood by the casket in both places to greet the thousands—his supporters and detractors alike—who shuffled past. Although it was 1973, the 1960s had not been played out and many of the young in the long lines had marched against Johnson in the streets. Lady Bird remembered "one young man, very bearded, who stood before me so stoically and he bowed slightly." "My apologies," he said to her. "It's alright," she told him, "he wanted to change things too." And that's the way I remember Lyndon Johnson as well: as a man who had the opportunity to change things in America and used it.

Former President Richard M. Nixon.

VI

TWO FORMER
PRESIDENTS
AT THE
CROSSROADS

President Nixon's continuing passionate interest in foreign policy and world affairs absorbs much of his time as a former president. He maintains his deep involvement in foreign affairs by meeting with heads of state. The role he has chosen as a former president and his concept of the ex-presidency reflect his concept of the presidency: One should use wisely the experience one has gained in life to foster peace and freedom in the world.

President Carter believes that an individual can make a difference in this world, especially a former president who can focus attention on a problem or, better yet, on a solution. There is life after the White House. Jimmy Carter is not the first former president who has demonstrated this, but he is proving that today the potential for public service in the post-presidential period is greater than ever before.

—John V. Brennan

—Steven H. Hochman

With Richard Nixon at San Clemente:
A Memoir of
His Post-Presidential Years

JOHN V. BRENNAN

During the White House years of my former boss, Richard Nixon, I was a Marine Corps aide. That means that I opened a lot of doors, I saluted a lot, I said "yes sir" a lot, and being a colonel, I had the pleasure of telling generals, "Your commander in chief asks . . ."

It was a pretty good life until August 7, 1974. I was at Washington's National Airport about to take a flight to New England when I was paged over the airport intercom. My secretary was calling to tell me that Julie Nixon Eisenhower had called; her father would announce his resignation of the presidency the next day and he wanted me to go to California with him.

So instead of heading for New England, I went back to the White House and two days later I got on a helicopter with the former president and Mrs. Nixon, said good-bye to the Fords, waved goodbye to "Disneyland East," flew out to Andrews Air Force Base, and boarded Air Force One. Enroute to California, the few of us on board were armed with one copy of the federal legislation covering former presidents. That is how we prepared ourselves for Mr. Nixon's transition into life as a former president.

Needless to say, the post-presidential staff was a little disorganized. During the first days at San Clemente, we were stymied by even trivial matters. Soon after we arrived in California, for example, Charles Lindbergh died and President Nixon wanted to write his condolences to Ann Morrow Lindbergh. But this act of kindness became a minor crisis because all the stationery at San Clemente had the presidential seal on it! So we traveled to the local stationery store to purchase needed office supplies.

Even a little thing like the mail became a major problem. It started piling up quickly after our arrival in San Clemente—first two bags, then five bags, and pretty soon there were twenty bags of mail to be answered. We soon realized that it was not going to stop; people were going to continue to write. So we contacted a local Republican women's club and we were blessed with forty volunteers who sorted the mail for us and did various clerical duties for the next few years.

Travel was another simple activity that became a major headache. I remember the first time that we left the San Clemente compound. I was very anxious about Mr. Nixon's transition from being a very powerful president of the United States to being an isolated former president. I remember that the president suggested that we leave the compound. "Let's go for a ride down the coast and we'll stop for lunch on the way back," he said.

To my continuing surprise, such a modest trip became a major logistical event. First we had to tell the Secret Service *what* we were going to do and *where* we were probably going to stop for lunch. They, in turn, sent agents ahead to go through the restaurant, clear the parking lot, and check out the men's room. Just as we entered the restaurant, I remember thinking that Mr. Nixon never carried money. "He's going to give me the usual instructions," I thought to myself. He usually said things like, "Now, Jack, tip generously and don't forget the wine steward; you always forget the wine steward." "Wine steward," I thought, "this is a fast-food joint!"

It was an interesting time, but we learned everything by doing. Eventually, we ended up running the office of a former president a lot like a business, a business without a profit-and-loss statement but with a budget.

Many people question whether the American taxpayers should be supporting former presidents who are more than able to provide for themselves and their families with personal resources. This is an on-going debate that I cannot resolve. I will make clear, however, how former President Nixon uses his share of the federal appropriation and conducts his business. His office allowance is used to cover the considerable cost of answering the mail and related activities; however, in 1984, Mrs. Nixon requested that there be no more Secret Service protection for her, and a year later, in 1985, Mr. Nixon did the same.

The Nixon presidential library will be the first that will be supported by private funds—not by taxpayers. Enough money was raised to build the structure and underwrite its operating costs. It opened in the summer of 1990 near Mr. Nixon's birthplace in Yorba Linda, California.

President Nixon is also very careful about remuneration for his private activities. The former president does not take honorariums for speeches or any other activity. This is not a new practice; he has not accepted an honorarium in thirty-five years. He does not sit on any boards. He does not lend his name as a consultant or adviser.

It is important to Mr. Nixon that he be able to travel and say the things he wants to say when he feels it appropriate. He wants to speak out when he thinks he can make an impact rather than because he needs or wants money. This is part of a desire on the part of the former president to remain active in world affairs. Since 1974 he has visited twenty-five countries and met with a number of heads of state including Mikhail Gorbachev and Deng Xio Peng; he has shared his views with many world leaders. He's written six books and in all of them he expresses views on a variety of subjects. He has written numerous articles and he speaks often to economic councils and foreign affairs councils around the country. In this way he influences public opinion and keeps himself informed on current affairs.

I recall how, during the Three Mile Island incident, the former president educated himself. As soon as he heard about Three Mile Island he was on the phone with physicist Edward Teller, finding out all he could. Teller would mention someone else, and President Nixon would call that person, and so on. By the end of the day he was almost an expert on the events at Three Mile Island. President Nixon follows that procedure with many issues in the news; he is intrigued by many everyday events.

President Nixon's continuing passionate interest in foreign policy and world affairs absorbs much of his time as a former president. He maintains his deep involvement in foreign affairs by meeting with heads of state. The role he has chosen as a former president and his concept of the ex-presidency reflect his concept of the presidency: One should use wisely the experience one has gained in life to foster peace and freedom in the world.

With Jimmy Carter in Georgia
A Memoir of
His Post-Presidential Years

STEVEN H. HOCHMAN

On September 11, 1989, *Time* magazine announced on its
cover, "Jimmy Carter Is Back." A related story was entitled
"Hail to the Ex-Chief." In large type it began, "Despite all
his troubles in the White House, Jimmy (yes, Jimmy Carter)
may be the best former President America has ever had."

The article described a man in action around the world:
in China, mediating between the leaders in Beijing and their
Tibetan subjects; in Panama, denouncing Manuel Noriega
for election fraud; in sub-Saharan Africa, helping to eradicate
disease or to persuade farmers to enlist in the Green Revolution; and in Atlanta at the Carter Center, convening negotiations between the government of Ethiopia and the Eritrean
People's Liberation Front.

As a member of President Carter's staff, I found this article
gratifying, but it also made me recall an earlier *Time* article
that was not so complimentary. The subtitle of the article
that appeared in May 1982 was: "Alone in Plains with
Rosalynn, his word processor and his woodshop."

To the Washington bureau chief who wrote this story it
seemed hard to understand how a former president could
return to a "rustic and provincial life" in a village of 651
people. He described his visit to the Carters' "strangely quiet
and dimly lit" ranch house, where President Carter received
him after working on his memoirs since before daybreak.
He found a man engrossed by his book and cut off from

123

the world. In terms of politics, Jimmy Carter had vanished from the earth: "Shunned by his fellow Democrats, ignored by his successor," he had become a "non-person, a President who never was."

Carter, according to the journalist, rarely left his house except for jogging, going to church, and attending "the funerals of old friends." Once every six weeks he would also go "to town" to get a haircut from "Norinne Lowell at the local barbershop."

People in Plains did not think much of this account. I remember Norinne complaining that she was a hairstylist, not a barber. I thought the article grossly inaccurate as well. To begin with, Jimmy Carter was not alone in Plains, just with Rosalynn, his word processor and his woodshop—I was there as well!

President Carter's so-called isolation was greatly exaggerated and misunderstood. To remind you—President Carter left the White House on January 20, 1981. Large crowds welcomed him home to Plains, but he immediately left for Wiesbaden, West Germany, where *he* welcomed back to freedom the Americans who had been held hostage in Iran.

I began working for him in Plains at the end of July to help him write his presidential memoirs. On August 9, Anwar Sadat, then president of Egypt, came to Plains accompanied by a large entourage, including the international media. A crowd of thousands came to town to witness the events. To prepare for this, everyone on President Carter's small staff was put to work, including me. I helped construct the podium.

Less than two weeks later, President Carter and his family headed to China and Japan and were gone for a little more than two weeks. A month after they returned, the prime minister of Israel, Menachem Begin, paid his visit to Plains. Again the tiny village had to accommodate thousands of people, and everyone available had to pitch in to help. I remember thinking during those first months that President Carter and I were not giving his memoirs the attention they needed if we were going to complete a manuscript in time to meet the publisher's deadline.

By the next spring, however, when the *Time* interview occurred, President Carter had radically adjusted his schedule and was concentrating intensely on the book. I learned that he had a remarkable ability to apply himself and to work long hours. I also learned that even when he was involved in a multitude of things, he was able to move from topic to topic and still focus on every item. In Plains he could isolate himself while he was writing. Also in Plains, he could find the tranquility that is so important for most writers.

Tranquility is not a word that President Carter especially uses. The former president who most talked about his need for tranquility was Thomas Jefferson. I had him on my mind because I had just finished assisting Dumas Malone with the sixth and final volume of his life of Thomas Jefferson. This work, *The Sage of Monticello*, is an account of Jefferson after his presidency. Naturally, I looked for similarities and differences between the two former presidents.

I did not know Jimmy Carter personally before he left the White House. I first met him in May 1981 in Atlanta where his post-presidential transition office had been established. I was being interviewed for the job of research assistant. The glamour of the presidency still seemed to surround Mr. Carter. His office in the federal building was impressive, and I was seated in the waiting room with former Secretary of State Dean Rusk, who was also there for an appointment.

The next month, however, I received a contrasting picture of the life of a former president. This time I joined President Carter in a drive down to Plains for a follow-up interview.

Contrary to popular notions, Plains is not a suburb of Atlanta; this trip was a three-hour drive through country fields and small towns. We stopped only once on the way, for supper at a fast food restaurant. The next morning, after President Carter offered me the job, he asked me to join him and Rosalynn in a visit to his mother at her house outside town; we would be picking blackberries in the woods. Near the house was a plum tree and President Carter climbed up to add that fruit to our collection. "Now you know what Jefferson did when he came home," President Carter observed to me.

That was exactly right. Upon leaving the presidency, Thomas Jefferson had spent nearly every day in his fields and gardens at Monticello. He was seeking tranquility, although his first priority had to be to get his personal affairs and finances in shape. He intentionally refrained from involvement in public affairs. He wanted his successor, James Madison, to stand on his own.

Jimmy Carter's return was similar. His finances were in bad shape—writing his memoirs quickly was important for that reason. The book he really wanted to write first was on the Camp David peace negotiations, but potential publishers wanted a full memoir of his administration. President Carter also thought it was appropriate to stay out of politics for some time and not be publicly critical of his successor. This was not the special decision of a defeated politician. It has been the general pattern for former presidents to cooperate in allowing a so-called honeymoon.

President Carter also wanted to devote his time to planning future activities. He was obligated to raise funds in order to build a presidential library. He had decided to affiliate with a university (quite a few were interested) and to develop some kind of institute through which he could continue to work for peace and human rights in the world. He wanted this next stage of his career to begin by the fall of 1982. Although Atlanta ultimately would be the site for his center and offices, it was natural for him to return home to Plains to live.

Former presidents who have homes almost always go home. This was true for George Washington, John Adams, and Thomas Jefferson, and it was also true for Harry Truman and Lyndon Johnson. Jimmy Carter's hometown of Plains is very small, but it is larger than Charlottesville was when Jefferson returned home. Plains is also the center of the Carter family.

Jimmy Carter is isolated there only when he chooses to be. Besides his access to modern communications devices—telephones, television, satellite dishes, and facsimile machines, among others, he is never far away from an airplane that can take him anywhere in the world. Technological advances in communications and transportation have had an enormous impact on the life of a former president. No one expected Thomas Jefferson to give newspaper interviews—there was no such practice at the time. Now President Carter receives frequent requests for interviews from journalists from every corner of the globe.

Thomas Jefferson never again left Virginia during the seventeen years he lived after his presidency. However, in October 1981, it seemed entirely appropriate to send former presidents Carter, Ford, and Nixon to Egypt as official American representatives at the funeral of President Anwar Sadat.

Former presidents today have many more opportunities to be involved in public life than former presidents had in the past—but they still have much in common with their predecessors. The happy ones are those who get on with their lives. Jimmy Carter, like Thomas Jefferson, always finds a new project to interest him. This has been true all his life. He saw writing his memoirs as a new challenge.

Instead of hiring a ghost writer or a team of researchers as other former presidents have done, he decided to write his own book. He believed that he did need someone with experience who could help him, and I was hired for that role. As we worked together, it became clear that I would be less involved with research than I had expected and more involved with helping to organize the book and seeing that the right questions were asked. The main sources for the book were Jimmy Carter's memory and his diary. He told me that we would leave the extensive documentary research to the historians. This approach was not easy for me at first because I was trained to conduct exhaustive documentary research. Although I found that President Carter recognized the need for research and accuracy, he was not consumed by it. He is fundamentally a man of action. He likes to get things done. He wants results.

The book President Carter wrote, *Keeping Faith: Memoirs of a President*, is his account of his presidency. Written in clear English—he calls it "peanut farmer language"—the book is easily accessible to readers and it became a best seller. Jimmy Carter did not try to be comprehensive; rather, he focused on a select group of issues, the ones with which he was most personally involved. Although President Carter is known as a detail man, the fact is that he delegates responsibility quite well. He believed, however, that some issues required the president to thoroughly understand them. The best known of these issues is the Middle East, and not surprisingly the section on this topic is the best part of his book.

The success of this first book led him to write others. *An Outdoor Journal* is an autobiographical account of his experiences in the outdoors. Earlier, he wrote *The Blood of Abraham*, which focuses on the search for peace between Israelis and Arabs in the Middle East. *Everything to Gain: Making the*

Most of the Rest of Your Life was written with his wife Rosalynn, who has continued to be an active partner in the post-presidential years. She also wrote her own memoirs, *First Lady From Plains*, which achieved number one ranking on the *New York Times* best-seller list.

Two of the books, *Blood of Abraham* and *Everything to Gain: Making the Most of the Rest of Your Life*, grew out of projects of the Carter Center of Emory University. During the first year after leaving the presidency, Jimmy Carter had decided what he wanted to do with the rest of his life. The key to this was the creation of a unique institution: the Carter Center. He wanted the center to be a place where he could bring people together to resolve differences. He recalled that after the Camp David negotiations between Israel and Egypt, he was inundated with requests of people in conflict that he take them to Camp David and mediate some kind of settlement. He knew there was a real need for an institution that could help to do this.

The Carter Center is linked to two other institutions. Built in conjunction with the Jimmy Carter Library and Museum, it is related to Emory University in Atlanta, where President Carter became University Distinguished Professor. Emory is an institution on the rise. In 1979 it had received the largest single gift ever contributed to a university. A foundation funded by Robert Woodruff of Coca-Cola had increased the university's endowment by $105 million. This placed the endowment among the top fifteen in the nation and gave the university the opportunity to make major improvements in its academic program.

President Carter's appointment began in September 1982. I joined him at the university, helping him with the adjustment to academic life. The time schedule of a university was strange to him, not only because of the academic calendar of semesters and summer vacations but also because of the long lead-time to which faculty members are accustomed. Administrators are used to dealing with researchers who develop their projects over many years. Both Jimmy Carter and Emory University had to learn to adjust.

President Carter chose not to be a conventional professor, teaching a graduate seminar or a lecture class and grading papers. In order to have the broadest impact on the university, he chose to teach in all the colleges and schools. Every month during the academic year, he devotes two or three days to lectures, forums, and meetings at the university. He begins in September with an annual town hall meeting held in the largest auditorium of the university. At that occasion he discusses any subject raised by students or faculty.

His regular lectures are on more specific topics. For instance, to a class on the history of U.S. foreign relations, he might lecture about the foreign policy of his administration. For a class on the history of the modern Near East he might discuss the Camp David accords. In the medical school and the law school, he regularly visits classes entitled "Human Values in Medicine" and "The Legal Profession." He draws upon his experiences as governor and president to discuss a wide variety of issues. In the theology school, he visits courses such as "Christian Ethics," where he discusses the challenge of maintaining public ethics.

In his teaching, President Carter draws on his current activities as well as those of his presidency. Even before ground was broken for the permanent facilities of the Carter Center, President Carter and Emory launched several programs for the institution. These and later programs focused on areas of special interest for President Carter, areas of accomplishment for his administration in which he believed he could continue to make a difference. The first project was to further the peace process in the Middle East. The second focused on international security and arms control. The third, entitled "Closing the Gap," examined the gap between what the United States knows how to do in health care and what it is actually achieving.

This period of experimentation for the Carter Center continues. Working within an academic community, Jimmy Carter is examining how his experience as a former president can be brought to bear on world problems. One of the initial projects have evolved programs headed by Fellows who are experts in their fields and who also teach at Emory. Students participate in programs as interns and volunteers.

Representing the Carter Center, President Carter travels widely. For the first Middle East project he went on a fact-finding mission through seven countries in the region, meeting not only with the heads of government in each country, but also with scholars, journalists, and local leaders. The nonpartisan nature of all the programs of the Carter Center is achieved by having bipartisan leadership.

President Carter learned early in his post-presidential career that his impact would be increased greatly by working closely with former President Gerald Ford. Their first joint venture was at the Gerald R. Ford Library on the University of Michigan campus in Ann Arbor. On February 9, 1983, they joined together for a session of the Domestic Policy Association. President Ford paid a visit to Emory University in November 1983 for the first Middle East consultation of the Carter Center. This session drew governmental representatives from Middle East nations as well as academic participants. The open and public discussion by both Arabs and Israelis was remarkable.

Other prominent Republicans, such as Henry Kissinger and Howard Baker, have joined President Ford and President

Carter for projects on international and domestic policy. The current U.S. administration has always been kept informed of activities.

The Carter Center entered a new stage on October 1, 1986, when the permanent facilities were dedicated and opened by President Ronald Reagan. The center was able to expand, and William Foege, M.D., assumed the position of executive director. An international leader in public health, he had orchestrated the eradication of smallpox in the world and served previously as director of the U.S. Centers for Disease Control. President Carter worked with Foege and Professor Norman Borlaug, who won the Nobel Peace Prize for his work on the Green Revolution in India and Pakistan, in launching an activist arm of the center called Global 2000. This organization has health and agricultural projects in Africa and Asia.

During a center consultation on the future of democracy in Latin America, President Carter assisted in the establishment of the Council of Freely-Elected Heads of Government. Established to assist emerging democracies in the hemisphere, this fourteen-member council includes current as well as former heads of state. It was as chairman of the council that President Carter went to Panama to monitor the election in 1989. In the same role, he recently monitored the election process in Nicaragua.

Another innovative program of the Carter Center is the International Negotiating Network (INN). Working with the Secretaries General of the United Nations, the British Commonwealth, and the Organization of American States, President Carter identified an unfilled role in dispute resolution; no organization existed to mediate intranational armed conflicts. International bodies are restricted by their charters from intervening in domestic disputes, yet ninety percent of all conflicts in the world are within nations rather than between nations. The first major effort of the INN has been to mediate the conflict between the government of Ethiopia and the Eritrean People's Liberation Front.

Jimmy Carter is not the first former president to serve in the academic world. Grover Cleveland was affiliated with Princeton, and William Howard Taft became a professor of law at Yale. A number of other former presidents have served on boards of trustees, but not since Thomas Jefferson created the University of Virginia has anyone created an institution as innovative as the Carter Center. Combining scholarship and action, the programs of the center have an exceptional impact because of the influence of a former American president. The University of Virginia was strikingly unique when it was founded by Jefferson. Through the years many of its characteristics have become the rule, rather than the exception, at other institutions of higher learning. In recent speeches to academic leaders, President Carter has urged that other American universities expand their active involvement in the Third World, providing assistance in all academic disciplines from agriculture to business, from public administration to medicine. He says that leaders of developing nations would welcome the help of nongovernment organizations in alleviating poverty and suffering. The practical experience gained by American faculty and students, he believes, would be of great benefit to us as well.

Numerous other activities of President Carter could be discussed. One that must be mentioned is Habitat for Humanity, an organization with which he and Rosalynn are especially involved. They have become a familiar sight on television, dressed in their work clothes, wielding hammers and saws, creating housing for the poor. President Carter believes that an individual can make a difference in this world, especially a former president who can focus attention on a problem or, better yet, on a solution.

There is life after the White House. Jimmy Carter is not the first former president who has demonstrated this, but he is proving that today the potential for public service in the post-presidential period is greater than ever before.

Former Presidents Gerald R. Ford and Jimmy Carter at the Ford Library.

VII

THE FUTURE
ROLE
OF FORMER
PRESIDENTS

While almost everyone agrees that we are not making full use of the knowledge, wisdom, and experience of former presidents, there have been few practical suggestions of what should be done. The one repeatedly suggested—that former presidents be given a nonvoting role in the House of Representatives and/or the Senate—has not been met with wide approval and has not been given serious consideration by the Congress. I do not join in the complaints of the ample financial and security provisions for former presidents. But the generous provision that the Congress and the American people have made suggests a widespread belief that former presidents should not cease to play a role in our public life.

—Daniel J. Boorstin

Saving a National Resource:
An Address on the Role
of Former Presidents
in American Public Life

DANIEL J. BOORSTIN

Our American strength, we have often been told, has been our youth. Ours is, or until recently was, a young nation. "The youth of America," Oscar Wilde observed nearly a century ago, "is their oldest tradition. It has been going on now for three hundred years." It was the young in spirit, we say, who had the strength and the will and the flexibility to leave an Old World, to risk an Atlantic or Pacific passage for the uncertain promises of a still-uncharted America. The framers of the Constitution provided that a person thirty-five years of age was old enough to be president, a senator needed to be only thirty, a member of the House of Representatives only twenty-five. The Twenty-sixth Amendment to the Constitution lowered the voting age to eighteen. We have been ingenious, too, in devising institutions—like our land grant colleges and the G.I. bill—to make the best use of our youth-resource.

But as our nation has matured—some would say only aged—as the need for immigrant courage is less general, and as life expectancy has increased, our population has been aging. And we have not shown the same enthusiasm and delight for old age. Our ingenuity in meeting the needs and opportunities and demands of youth has not been matched by any similar ingenuity in devising institutions to employ our older population. The late Senator Claude Pepper did a great service by focusing concern on the needs of the

139

elderly. Though we have provided Golden Eagle passes for senior citizens to the national parks, we have run into gross political problems trying to provide health insurance especially for our aging citizens. The most conspicuous American institution directed to senior citizens is the so-called leisure city, a place not of creation but of recreation and vegetation. Our concern for the special needs of our ailing, idle, and disoriented aged has been admirable. But we need to refocus our attention on how to employ the special talents and resources of our most experienced citizens.

This contemporary view of aging has had an impact on the role of former presidents in American public life. We now have four living former presidents, all happily functioning and in good health. This, I think, is a near record. In 1861 the number of living former presidents (Van Buren, Tyler, Fillmore, Pierce, and Buchanan) came to five. The number of living former presidents is likely to increase, with the decline in smoking and the increasing longevity of the American population and especially since the passage of the Twenty-second Amendment to the Constitution, which prevents a president from serving more than two terms.

The television spotlight on the sitting president has somehow deepened the penumbra into which a former president falls when he is no longer in the White House. Television has given a new meaning to the old proverb, "Out of sight, out of mind." Our failure to create a role in public life for former presidents is partly a reflection of our American preoccupation with youth, another symptom of our chronic ineptness in providing productive roles for older citizens.

One of the most distinctive and uncelebrated features of our American presidency has helped create the problem of the "castaway president." The fixed four-year term makes a president's tenure different from that of a prime minister in a parliamentary system who can be turned out of office on short notice by a parliamentary majority or similarly brought back for a short period. Our fixed term has allowed our presidents to stay in office even when they have outlived their popularity with the electorate and even though they have no majority in either house of Congress. The fixed term has thus given a prudent stability to the office. Because the Twenty-second Amendment makes every president a lame duck in his second term, the constitutionally fixed term seems also to have defined a terminus to a president's active role in public life. A president, like other former holders of high office, is in danger of becoming what in Washington is called "a former person."

While almost everyone agrees that we are not making full use of the knowledge, wisdom, and experience of former presidents, there have been few practical suggestions of what should be done. The one repeatedly offered—that former presidents be given a nonvoting role in the House of Representatives and/or the Senate—has not met wide approval and has not been given serious consideration by the Congress. I do not join in the complaints of the ample financial and security provisions for former presidents. But the generous provision that Congress and the American people have made suggests a widespread belief that former presidents should not cease to play a role in our public life.

I would like to offer a suggestion—perhaps only the skeleton of a suggestion. Perhaps we have an opportunity to begin to find a way to fill a lacuna in our institutions. Perhaps at the same time that we offer a new role for our former presidents, we can find a way to bring more prominently into the public forum Americans of wisdom and experience in all fields.

Our American need was dramatized for me when I was living in England and following parliamentary debates as reported in the London *Times*. I was not the only one to notice the superiority of the debates in the House of Lords over those in the House of Commons. The House of Lords, the unelected but elite second chamber of the British legislature, has little legislative power despite its antiquity and prestige. But it has changed its character in recent years. Its hereditary membership has been overshadowed by the persons appointed for their recognized distinction and leadership in all areas of British life.

The House of Lords has come to include economists like Barbara Ward, historians like Hugh Thomas and Asa Briggs, and scientists like chemist Frederick Dainton. These people have earned public respect and their right to be heard on public issues by their signal achievement in their special fields. Yet in the past they have had only the forum of their professional specialty—except for random interviews in the press, radio, and television incited less by public need than by the desire of the media to fill space or time. Now that the character of the British second chamber has been changing, these people have a forum where they can join in publicized debate on major public issues and where they can raise issues that they think have been neglected.

An additional qualification for membership in this group, important for us to note, is withdrawal from the pursuit of elective office. This has made it an appropriate place, too, for former prime ministers, who are among the body's most valuable members.

It occurred to me to ask myself, and then to ask others, whether somehow we could devise an American institution, within our democratic tradition and our constitutional frame, to give us the benefits of a similar national forum. Obviously, heredity and aristocracy have no place in our country. But we too can benefit from a wider forum on national issues for our most experienced leaders in labor, business, science, literature, education, and the arts—for our citizens who have never been politicians or have ceased to be politicians. Without authorization from anybody, I have discussed this possibility during the past few years with a number of our leading citizens. I have found nearly unanimous agreement that there is something missing from our public life.

What I offer, then, is perhaps nothing more than the skeleton of an idea to stir our thinking toward creating a new national institution. National network television, with its auxiliaries in the cables and the facilities of VHS, has provided unprecedented facilities for bringing together, on the screen and in living rooms, speakers who remain in widely separated places, and for allowing their words and ideas to reach unprecedented numbers. Now our nation can witness the exchanges of opinion and share the wisdom and experience of our best qualified leaders, not merely on political issues. As a forum, television is presently used for formal occasions, like the inauguration of a president or a campaign debate with its countless casual interviews and encounters. Has not the time come to use this unprecedented technology for an unprecedented forum of leading and experienced Americans? Is it not time to give rhythm and regularity to such a forum, where citizens can follow the points of view of different leading Americans continuously and through time?

Our effort here to discuss and define a role for former presidents is providential—for now our living former presidents could provide a core of a new national council, a House of Experience. And at the same time they could answer an initial question: Who will name the first members of the council? Perhaps each living former president could be asked to name three persons to join the group, which would bring the number to sixteen, for the present. Former chief justices of the Supreme Court and, perhaps, former speakers of the House of Representatives could be added. Later, the group as a whole could be responsible for filling vacancies or adding members.

How often, where, and how should this national council of experience meet? There are many possibilities, and the proper rhythm and frequency of meetings will appear when the group has begun to meet. To accomplish the purpose, to provide a continuing forum and continuing public interest, the meetings should be regular and not too infrequent. Perhaps the group could gather at least once a year either in Washington or at one of the presidential libraries. Other meetings could bring together some of the members as a committee and the whole group could, on a quarterly basis, exchange ideas through a televised forum from their separate places.

Who should set the agenda? Who is better qualified to help us focus on enduring national issues than our former presidents with their experience and their feeling for the nation's unfinished business? What sorts of topics should be on the agenda? The council members would decide, but it seems to me that the spotlight should be on long-term problems (such as education, the relation of the United States to other countries and the world, the role and status of the family in American life, and the environment) rather than on current questions of policy. The success of this national council would be seen in its ability to focus the experience and wisdom of leaders who are not seeking votes on matters of long-term national concern and on its ability to awaken interest in questions not in the headlines.

How could such a group be created? There are many possibilities. One would be an act of Congress chartering the council as a nonprofit institution similar to the act chartering the American Historical Association. The national council should have no legal authority and no legislative role. It would be chartered to meet, discuss, and explore in public view the nation's long-term concerns.

All these specifics are only suggestions. Many other possibilities will occur to you. I am persuaded that we have here an unprecedented opportunity created by our technology and an unprecedented core resource in our former presidents. With your imagination and knowledge, with their wisdom and experience, and with the help of others we may be able to begin to fill a need in our public life.

Former Presidents
in American Public Life:
A Symposium

Robert H. Ferrell:

The role for former presidents—so it seems to me—should be to symbolize American democracy. They should constantly bear in mind that they once represented the majesty of their high office, but that official majesty did not extend to themselves.

Consider the behavior of two presidents who held this point of view. Harry S. Truman liked to say that when people came to see him, they came to pay their respects to the office, not to see Harry Truman. Sometimes they fawned over him in ways that embarrassed him. He always sought to understand their confusion. Washington, he believed, was part of the trouble. He liked to joke about "Potomac fever." He said it was a sudden, virulent, highly contagious disease. After a feverish visitor left the Oval Office he sometimes inquired of his personal physician, Dr. Wallace Graham, whether so-and-so was showing signs of illness, and Wally would gravely agree that the symptoms of the fever were there.

I once met Truman and learned a lesson in democracy. He was wearing his double-breasted suit and perhaps a scrambled-egg tie. He came up, put out his hand, and said, "Truman." In one of the minor anticlimaxes of the present century I put out mine and said, "Ferrell."

Another president who felt the same way about the office of president of the United States was Calvin Coolidge, whose memory is not now as green as that of Truman. If someone asked to shake Coolidge's hand he would simply extend it like a limp dishrag, and the visitor could shake it if he wished —all the while the president would be talking to someone else.

Coolidge also helped keep his head by dispensing Vermont witticisms. In his antediluvian time the Washington press corps consisted of perhaps half a dozen reporters who came to his press conferences. (Incidentally, he often denoted these fellows as "the class.") A member of the class once asked him if he was going up to the Sesquicentennial Exposition in Philadelphia. The presidential answer—actually that of "the White House spokesman" (Coolidge never allowed direct quotation)—was "yes." "Why are you going, Mr. President?" asked the reporter. "As an exhibit," was the answer.

Our European friends have often remarked that Americans are basically as antidemocratic as anyone else. They point to the American love of titles; they mention the elaborate automobiles, the show of dress styles. One need not add to this list to say that they nonetheless understand the reality of American democracy and, if they themselves are not at the top of their social heap, they admire it. Again, so it would seem, a retired president can demonstrate how the country was built on equality of opportunity, he can testify not that anyone can be president, for that is not true, but that all Americans can aspire to the office.

A retired president can urge policies based on his experience, serve on committees and commissions, travel around the country and satisfy the curious (that is, go as an exhibit). The basic purpose of his remaining years, however, should be to show that he came from Staunton, Blooming Grove, Plymouth Notch, West Branch, Independence, Abilene, or Grand Rapids, that momentarily he assumed the office, but that the office never consumed him.

Gerald R. Ford:

I have mixed emotions about a council of former presidents. From time to time I have read of other proposals to establish such a group, but I have not been persuaded it was a good idea. In general, I am critical of these proposals because they will lead to the establishment of another bureaucracy in Washington. As you might guess, I have a serious reservation about any more bureaucracy being imposed on the banks of the Potomac!

These proposals are very well intentioned, but I am concerned about the relationship of a council of former presidents to the other institutions in Washington. What would be the relationship between the Congress and this new council? The Congress does not need any more problems; they manufacture enough for themselves!

And what would be the relationship between the incumbent president and this council? In late 1987 it was proposed that former President Carter and I undertake an in-depth study of our national issues and make recommendations to the new president to be elected in 1988. We enlisted about eight very prominent Democrats and an equal number of prominent Republicans on the committee and the final report came to be called the *American Agenda*. It made specific proposals involving economic policy, domestic policy, foreign policy, and defense and arms control policies. It was a very sizable document and, in my judgment, it was extremely well done. It was put together by some of the best minds in various disciplines, and we are very proud of the document.

President Carter and I made a special trip to Washington to discuss the report with then President-elect Bush. He accepted it, but made no comment. I do not think that Mr. Bush was hostile to the report, but I did feel an adverse reaction from his staff. And you know what happens to a document if the staff does not like it: It never sees the light of day! As far as I know, very few of these proposals ended up in any of the recommendations of the newly elected president. Maybe a formal council would have a better track record. I must say, however, that I was somewhat disappointed with the reaction to the *American Agenda* because a lot of good people aside from President Carter and myself took the time to make constructive proposals.

What should former presidents do? It is my personal opinion that we cannot and should not define a rigid role for former presidents. We are all different and I think that will be the case in the future. My own preference is that a former president's relationship to the presidential office or the people in charge of the government be informal and personal. If a former president has a strong opinion about an issue, whether it is foreign policy or domestic policy, there is no problem in getting access to any governmental official. I had excellent access to President Carter when he was in office and I had the same with President Reagan. I probably have the best relationship with President Bush. It is very easy to make that personal contact. I believe, from substantial experience, that personal contact has a greater impact on a president in office than the massive effort that President Carter and I made through the *American Agenda*.

I also believe that presidents in office feel more comfortable in contacting their predecessors without going through the bureaucracy. And I know from some practical experience that is the case. Although President Carter and I had few comparable views on domestic policy, we did share a reasonably good agreement on foreign policy. In four specific cases, at President Carter's request, I was helpful in trying to pass his proposals in the Senate. I had a somewhat similar relationship with President Reagan; he could call and ask for help when he needed it. And certainly George Bush and I have the same relationship.

In summary then, I tilt against a council of former presidents because of my traditional opposition to more bureaucracy; because there is no impediment to a former president's access to his successors; and because we are all different to some extent and would not necessarily be a cohesive body in a formalized commission or committee.

Roger Mudd:

It seems to me that the day a president becomes a former president he becomes a former president—not a former president without a portfolio or a former president at large or a former president in loco presidentis. That is, he becomes a citizen again—albeit a distinguished and perhaps even a respected one—but a citizen without any constitutional or statutory or bequeathed powers or responsibilities.

Certainly, former presidents should have an influence on their country's public policy, on their own political parties, and on their countrymen. But that influence, it seems to me, ought to be based on their reputations, accomplishments, wisdom, believability and political credibility, and not on any power bestowed upon them by law. In addition, the influence of former presidents should be applied by the former presidents themselves—through books, speeches, articles—and not through any formalized channels created and established by the government.

It is my belief that when a president leaves office through defeat, the American public has sent a very strong message that it found him lacking and wants to be free of him; and when a president retires after two terms the American public is entitled to or is looking forward to being free of him.

I also think a new president is entitled to be free of his predecessor. The new headmaster does not want Mr. Chips living on campus. I shudder to think of the political agony President Ford would have gone through back in 1974–1975 if he had been required to consult or brief his predecessor or appoint him as foreign policy negotiator plenipotentiary. And if I may say so, I suspect Jimmy Carter would have found another way to skin the cat before submitting to a law requiring him to make his predecessor an ex-officio member of his Domestic Policy Council. In other words, I think that as a government we ought not be making any more use of our former presidents than we make now.

That is not to suggest that incumbents should not tap excumbents for advice, fact-finding, or occasional diplomatic missions, or that former presidents should never darken the White House door. Without question, Harry Truman had good instincts when he tapped Herbert Hoover to run a commission on the reorganization of the executive branch; but Hoover had been out of office for twelve years. And most importantly, President Truman was not required to invite former President Hoover to serve. It was voluntary and at Truman's initiative, based on Hoover's reputation and standing and on Truman's reading of the political map.

It is my belief that presidents and former presidents do what is comfortable and appropriate for both. I think it has been the government's recent generosity in providing office space, office staff, office expense, pensions, and 24-hour-a-day protection that has created the impression that there is such a thing called the "Office of the Honorable Former President of the United States." Because we spend in excess of $12 million a year providing for and protecting former presidents and their families, some have suggested that we ought to be thinking up things for them to do so we feel we're getting our money's worth.

It seems to me one of the most effective ways for former presidents to be a valuable and positive force in the democracies to which they have contributed so much is through their libraries and museums and associated programs and forums. Such institutions and events can be educational, inspirational, dignified, and provocative. I must confess, however, that I pity the poor graduate student in twentieth-century presidential history who must fly from West Branch to Hyde Park to Independence to Abilene to Boston to Austin to Yorba Linda to Ann Arbor to Atlanta and back to Thousand Oaks.

Finally, I would observe that most Americans are naturally curious about their former presidents. It is hard to mainline on a single leader for four to eight years and then quit him cold turkey. But Americans are curious in a way that is not destructive. They want to know how he is doing, what he is doing, whether he is happy, whether he is readjusting gracefully, and maybe even what he thinks from time to time. But being curious doesn't mean they want him back in power.

Most Americans do not begrudge their former presidents a comfortable retirement; in fact, they would be embarrassed were it otherwise. But many wonder, I think, why they are asked to spend between $9 and $10 million a year to protect our former presidents on private $2-million trips to Japan and on $25,000 speaking engagements. Most Americans, it seems to me, think the country's care and feeding of former presidents is roughly about right and that perhaps if former presidents were all that crucial to the nation's future they might not be former presidents.

Helen Thomas:

I have often wondered why a sitting president—no matter what the party—has rarely solicited the help of former presidents. Why are these men figuratively put out to pasture? The one exception in my experience was Dwight Eisenhower. Ike's successors paid homage to him because he was in a class by himself—the "Great White Father." When Lyndon Johnson wanted Ike's blessing, Mohammed went to the mountain: LBJ flew to Palm Springs and landed on Ike's golf course. The same was true of John Kennedy when he wanted the Eisenhower aura.

At times, presidents have asked their predecessors to rally to a particular cause—to speak out and lend their voices and prestige to a view the White House was pushing—but not often. Presidents are notorious for not being fond of their predecessors. I don't know whether sitting presidents are jealous of their prerogatives or feel competitive, but they do not ask for advice from those who have been there before them. I think that is a shame because former presidents could become involved and put their oars in to help their successors. So visits by former presidents to their old haunt— the White House—are few and far between.

This is not to imply that former presidents are waiting by their telephones with nothing to do. In fact, they seem to be very busy. There are a number of constructive activities to engage former presidents. Thought-provoking seminars at presidential libraries can educate the public on important issues of the day; and as we have seen, former presidents can mediate international disputes as international observers.

What role should former presidents play in advising their successors? Ronald Reagan consulted Richard Nixon on foreign policy issues and also on several other undisclosed matters when he was running for reelection in 1984. But, as I have said before, most former presidents are not interested in their predecessors' view or skills. I think Harry Truman's use of Herbert Hoover's talents was the exception rather than the rule.

I would not accord a former president a seat in Congress

unless he ran and won it as John Quincy Adams did after he left the White House. The testimony and experience of former presidents is not for naught; they don't really need a structured forum as long as they have access to the media.

Some critics have questioned whether the press has been too critical of former presidents, but I think not. If anything, the complaint should be that former presidents are too often ignored when they have something to say. But we journalists are working on improving that state of affairs. The proper role of former presidents, therefore, is difficult to define. In truth, it will be up to each former president to shape his own unique role.

Francis H. Heller:

There is an appealing simplicity in Daniel Boorstin's suggestion of a "council of experience," with the surviving former presidents at its core. The analogy to the modern House of Lords is inviting as is the notion that, as a matter of course, the American people would not only listen to this small and select group but heed its advice.

But America is not England. The House of Lords, however much it has been transformed in the course of this century, speaks with the voice of tradition and, for a multiplicity of reasons, Englishmen have always shown interest in intellectual discourse while Americans have preferred to look for action rather than words. The likelihood of sessions of a small elite group attracting the interest of a nationwide television audience is open to debate. As one who rarely watches more than the late evening news on television, I suspect that the only way the public will be drawn to a presentation of the proceedings of the proposed council would be by the promise of shouting matches and fisticuffs.

Key to Boorstin's proposal is the presence of the former

presidents on the council he would like to see established. But as President Ford has demonstrated by his relation of the fate of the *American Agenda* report, incumbent presidents are rarely receptive to advice offered by their predecessors. Every new president comes into office with the promise that his administration will do things better than those that went before—even if it is no more than the promise to be "kinder and gentler." I suggest that it is in the nature of the office that each new administration has to be a new beginning. There is, in other words, an institutional impediment against the proposed organization of advice.

In his recent book *In the Shadow of FDR*, William Leuchten-burg has shown brilliantly that it is not only the immediate predecessor whose shadow hangs threateningly over his successors but also that of earlier chief executives, if their tenure is favorably remembered by a significant proportion of the public. If the new president is of a different party, his campaign will likely have focused on the shortcomings (if not the misdeeds) of the one he replaced.

We know how strongly Dwight D. Eisenhower felt about Harry S. Truman—he never asked his advice and it is unlikely that he would have acted on any advice that might have come to him from Independence, Missouri. Yet we also know that, especially in the area of foreign policy, there was not much difference in the views of the two men. Their animosity grew almost entirely out of the harshness of the campaign. Eisenhower deeply resented Truman's attacks on him (and eventually reciprocated in kind) while Truman, the professional politician, believed that he was not doing anything that was not part and parcel of traditional political campaigning. He never quite understood why Eisenhower got so upset about it.

We also know that Eisenhower resented Lyndon Johnson's use of him for what he, Eisenhower, believed were partisan purposes. William Ewald relates how furious Ike was when, after the president had asked to confer with him privately about issues relating to the Vietnam War, Johnson announced publicly that he had met with Eisenhower and received his advice.

Those of us in the academic world know that the kindest thing a former president or dean can do for his successor is to get out of town, even if it is only for a year's sabbatical. In the business world it is taken for granted that a former chief executive officer will leave the organization—and, if he does not, will keep his nose out of its affairs. Yet one might argue that former deans are a valuable resource for their schools and former CEOs for their corporations. What this suggests is that the harnessing of the resource presented by "formers" flies in the face of human nature.

I seriously doubt that these impediments, the institutional and the human one, can be overcome by the creation of an added structure, such as the suggested council of experience. The history of human government is full of examples of political and legal structures that, once established, develop into something never anticipated by their creators. Indeed the presidency itself has come to be something quite different from the image projected in the Constitutional Convention. We should think twice before we institutionalize the potential of counsel that may be provided by our former presidents. I am content to let its utilization grow out of the personal relationships between incumbents and their precursors.

Steven H. Hochman:

I recently asked President Carter whether he believed that the U.S. government could make better use of its former presidents by creating some kind of formal role for them. His response to my question was almost exactly the same

156

as that of President Ford to the question about a council of former presidents. Mr. Carter said that presidents have different natures and different motivations. To his thinking, we should not attempt to institutionalize the role of the former president; he is happy with things as they are. He did add, however, that he thought it appropriate that former presidents be kept informed by succeeding administrations, as he had kept President Ford and President Nixon informed.

This was not initially the case when Mr. Carter left office. He has said on occasion that he had no relationship with President Reagan during Reagan's presidency. However, some communication was established with the various secretaries of state and national security advisers. With President Bush, communication has been excellent. This has enabled President Carter to increase his effectiveness in working throughout the world for human rights and peace.

It seems to me that former presidents are most effective when they avoid partisan politics. Early in 1983, President Ford invited President Carter to the Ford library for a conference on public policy and they worked very well together on that occasion. That conference started something: They learned that they could be very effective together when speaking on issues of common concern. This relationship has continued at both the Ford and Carter libraries. When President Ford has not been able to work with Mr. Carter on a particular conference at the Carter Center, Mr. Carter has always invited high-level Republicans to participate. Leadership is bipartisan and the conference or the program is nonpartisan.

Because of his prestige as a former president, Mr. Carter has been able to draw together the leading experts and policymakers on such issues as the conflict in the Middle East, international health policy, hunger in Africa, and the prospects for democracy in Latin America. Bringing together antagonists to talk peacefully in an academic setting has sometimes been the best he could achieve. But his objective is always to bring about substantial improvement in the lives of human beings. He has had many successes—increasing agricultural output in Africa, reducing disease in Asia and Africa, and building homes for the needy throughout the world.

Presidents of the United States get enormous amounts of attention. Hundreds of members of the press corps are always covering their activities, but when a president leaves the White House and goes back to Plains or wherever, the press seem to disappear. Recent former presidents are living happy productive lives. If they continue to be interested in public affairs, they have ample opportunity to contribute to their nation and the world.

Daniel J. Boorstin:

This is not so much a rebuttal as a way of listing suggestions. Since I have been living in Washington for a number of years, I am just as wary of bureaucracy as President Ford. But I am also wary of the bureaucratic fallacy that can corrupt us in the other parts of our lives. Our country has been ingenious in all kinds of inventions including institutional inventions; even our constitution is an invention, an unprecedented one. I cannot help thinking of the motto that was on the desk of a French civil servant: "Never do anything for the first time." I get some echoes of that in some of the comments of my colleagues.

We have here a wonderful resource of people who have impeccable credentials of experience and I think we should try to use this opportunity not only to provide more fruitful and open avenues for former presidents to share their experience but also to improve public television, commercial television, or any kind of television we can get it on. We should try to shame the networks into doing this if they will not do it for any other reason. I think there are so many different ways of organizing television programs and there is so much money in it I do not see any reason why it cannot be done.

I do share President Ford's wariness of bureaucracy. I do not imagine a numerous secretariat for this group, but I do think it useful to have an executive secretary, someone who could bring the group together. In this council we have an opportunity to do what representative government does best. Representative government is eventually a group of people exchanging ideas and developing in ways not possible for direction for a community that cannot be done by one or two people individually making statements. The need for the discourse of people in relation to each other is itself the axiom on which representative government is based.

I also believe that while each of our former presidents has a special kind of experience to offer, all of them together exchanging ideas in the public presence will add more than the sum of their individual talents. We would be able to compare their approaches to problems. I also think that it would be a way of inducing some of our wiser and experienced nonpoliticians to participate in such a forum. We could all think of people who would be selected by our former presidents to focus on long-term issues.

I do not think we should be worried now over finding a national agenda for this council. I do not think that we should imply that these former presidents or that those whom they enlist in the national council of experience should come up with legislative proposals. That is not their role; they should spark our thinking and encourage our reflection. And this is a service for which we should use our new technology and our almost unprecedented resource of presidential wisdom to help us.

My concern in my proposal is to refocus our attention on former presidents as a resource. I think that regardless of political party, former presidents can supply experience in our country which has not valued experience as much as we should. I would hope that we would find some way to use the wisdom of our former presidents.

DISCUSSION

Roger Mudd: President Ford, if a way was found to televise the discussion of a national council once or twice a year, would you feel comfortable sitting down with Ronald Reagan, Richard Nixon, Jimmy Carter, Warren Burger, and Jim Wright?

Gerald R. Ford: I would feel comfortable doing it, but I do not think it would be a very popular show on television. Personally, I do not find these types of programs to be very stimulating and they are rarely watched by the public. Even I think they are pretty boring. As far as *doing* it I would have no hesitancy. I think you would find some legitimate differences among members of the same political party as well as several differences between Republicans and Democrats. You would have some differences, but whether or not such debates would be appealing to the public is an open question.

Roger Mudd: Do you think it would, in fact, raise the level of public discourse?

Gerald R. Ford: I believe all of the participants would try to do that, and all of them would have specific areas where they wanted to make a point, whether they agreed or disagreed with the others. You could get some thoughtful discussion but I am not sure of very popular comments. Some of it might be pretty dull.

Helen Thomas: I disagree with President Ford that there would not be an audience for such a program. I think it would be tremendous to have four former presidents batting ideas around. You make a lot of speeches, President Ford, so obviously you think there is an audience out there. You obviously want to make an impact. I think the people would gain from such a program and there would be an audience for it.

Gerald R. Ford: I do not think the so-called debates among Democrats or among Republicans have much of a public audience. Maybe statistics tell a different story. I think these debates just end up being shouting matches. If we were to debate, I hope the four former presidents would set an example of getting along together.

Daniel J. Boorstin: That may be one of the main distinctions. These debates would not be in an electoral context. The former presidents would not be seeking votes; they would be trying to persuade people to their views in the long-term interests of the nation.

Steven H. Hochman: There are existing organizations similar to the one in this proposal. President Ford gathers a group of former heads of state on a regular basis in Vail, Colorado, and both President Carter and President Ford are members of the Council of Freely Elected Heads of Government, which concentrates on encouraging democracy in the western hemisphere. When Presidents Ford and Carter monitored the election in Panama last year [1989], for example, they went as members of that organization. These two presidents meet together frequently and speak publicly on issues of common concern. Their joint presentations are often televised on the public and cable television networks. I think these sessions are very worthwhile. They draw a good audience, but not of the size the major networks demand.

Gerald R. Ford: I get very few letters involving what either President Carter or myself said or discussed on such programs. We get plenty of mail otherwise, do not get me wrong. We get quite a few letters urging us to get active in specific causes; we get lots of advice on how we ought to comment on this subject or another; and we get many requests to give speeches, participate in events, and so forth. I probably turn down at least ten invitations for every one I accept, if not more. And I am sure President Carter has the same experience.

Roger Mudd: I think that former presidents should be encouraged to talk about current policy. It seems to me if you want a lively television show, you must include discussion of the issues that are before the nation: drugs and crime, for example. Without discussion of current policy, you eliminate the potential for having a lively talk about things that are most on people's minds.

Daniel J. Boorstin: I think there is very little danger that we will preclude our former presidents from talking about anything they want to talk about. That's encouraging; let them talk about what's in the public's interest.

Don W. Wilson: Let me add that meetings between two or more former presidents are special events worthy of television. In 1983, the Ford Library hosted a conference on domestic policy that brought President Carter and President Ford publicly together for the first time after they had left office, and it was an electric experience. Everybody in the room was captivated and the response was fantastic. The students and the professors at the University of Michigan, in almost unanimous chorus, said that it was one of the most significant events in their lives. I think it was the presence of the two of them together and the interaction and the interchange that made it so important. That was a dynamic event and one that I would hope we would find some mechanism for encouraging. Maybe the presidential libraries can serve that function.

Stephen E. Ambrose: As President Ford indicated, former presidents do not have any trouble getting a forum and can make their views known to the public when they wish. The difficulty that I have with this proposal is that some former presidents feel the need to defend their reputations, to run for the ultimate office—their place in history. It is very difficult to get former presidents out of politics!

What I found appealing about the proposal is the bringing together of the wise men, and they are not all in politics. Would it not have been marvelous if we could have had national discussions thirty years ago, in which George C. Marshall and Robert Oppenheimer sat down with some of the top men in the country from out of politics to discuss major issues looking into the near-term future?

One of the problems with politics is that what politicians want to talk about often has very little to do with the real movements that are taking place in the country and in the world. I am not sure that former politicians are the people we ought to be listening to on the issues that we are facing as we look toward the twenty-first century.

Daniel J. Boorstin: I am grateful to Stephen Ambrose for that suggestion. I do not think it would be amiss for the American public to hear former presidents defending their places in history rather than defending the positions of their political parties. I think if they tended to do that, that it would be good. I also am very glad, because it was part of my suggestion, that it be a council of wise men and women. I prize the opportunity of having so many former presidents, alive and vigorous, who could be charged with selecting nonpolitical persons who could form this council to discuss the long-term problems of the country.

Helen Thomas: I think that people who get to be former presidents can rise above themselves and make a contribution to the public debate on national issues. It does not matter if it is partisan. It is a contribution, and through the give-and-take, these former presidents can learn things. Former presidents have experienced something that very few people in this country have, or ever will. What they can do for young people is tremendous.

Gerald R. Ford: I do not disagree with that, but I do not want to institutionalize, formalize the process. The capability to speak out on issues depends on one's interests and the available forums. There is no problem whatsoever in my case in having an opportunity to either go to the Congress, and talk to Democrats and Republicans, or to go to the White House to see the president.

Helen Thomas: I do not think the idea is to restrict a former president's freedom of movement or action or anything else.

Every once in a while, people who are in this exclusive club of former presidents should get together and discuss the issues of the day. I really think that it would be fascinating.

Roger Mudd: When I first began to think about the role of former presidents in American life, all I could think of was that evening about five or six years ago when Jimmy Carter, Gerald Ford, and Richard Nixon appeared at the head table of the testimonial dinner for Hyman Rickover. The picture was widely printed all over the country of these three former presidents sitting together. About three nights later, at the Gridiron dinner, Robert Dole, who was one of the speakers that night said, "Did you see that picture in the paper the other day? There they were, Carter, Ford, and Nixon: see no evil, speak no evil, and evil."

Daniel J. Boorstin: I would like to add one final comment. My wife and I had the good fortune to know W. H. Auden, one of the great poets of this century, who became an American citizen. I remember it was the night before one of the Eisenhower-Stevenson elections, and Auden commented: "Do you know what's the most amazing thing about American political life?" "No," I said, "what's that?" "Neither candidate is packing his bags tonight," he responded. The civility of American political life, of which this discussion is an example, is something that we should explore and cultivate.

Former President Gerald R. Ford.

AFTERWORD

History offers little in the way of tradition. I have known seven former presidents personally. If you look at their activities after leaving office, you will be hard put to find a common pattern. What we do as former presidents is very much a matter of personal choice. To be sure, there are occasional obligations or expectations. But, in the main, what I have done since leaving the White House has been by my own choice and that is the way it ought to be. Frankly, I do not see the value in formalizing the role of former presidents. Historical circumstance, personal experience, and aptitude conspire against predetermined roles. Let former presidents decide what interest to pursue, what contributions to make, on their own.

—Gerald R. Ford

Personal Reflections on My Experiences as a Former President

GERALD R. FORD

I am pleased to carry a card in what Herbert Hoover called "my exclusive trade union" of former presidents. Yet there is irony in my status as a former president. I did not seek out the office of president. My political ambition was speaker of the House. Even as vice president, I did not expect to become president until only a few days before Richard Nixon's resignation in August 1974. The truth is, I wish there had never been a need for Spiro Agnew to resign and there had never been a Watergate. Although I was the beneficiary, Betty and I would have been very happy with the life we had laid out after my planned retirement from the House of Representatives at the end of 1976. Nevertheless, I became president. And frankly, once there, I hoped to have a few more years than I did to contemplate life after the White House.

I was disappointed to lose the 1976 election. It is the only election I have ever lost in politics, and, naturally, I thought the best man with the best policies had lost. But I reconciled myself to the fact that we had done our best; that we had run a good campaign. I was prepared to face the change in circumstances straightforwardly.

People frequently ask me whether I would have done something differently in that campaign. I answer that I do not spend much time looking back. I have competed enough in life and, whether it is athletics or politics or law, I know that sometimes you win and sometimes you lose. I have never felt that when you lose you should spend a lot of time with self-doubt. Life in the future is always something I look forward to—I do not like to live in the past. The attitude that out of disappointment comes new opportunity has guided me in the years since 1977.

This is not to say that it was easy to leave the White House. You cannot help but miss the presidency. I could never understand those who did not like it. I missed the opportunity to make decisions. Betty and I loved the daily challenges in the White House, and we enjoyed the responsibilities. But, once it was over, we found other very productive and interesting things to do.

Leaving the "pressure cooker on the Potomac" also allowed Betty and me to do some fun things just for us—like planning our home in Palm Springs. I took advantage of my new-found freedom from schedules to work on my golf game and ski in Vail, Colorado. I won't tell you what my handicap was that first summer, but if I could have substituted it for my electoral vote, I would have been president for four more years!

The time on the links paid off in a way it never did while I was in government. After sixty-four years, less than six months after I left office, I scored my first hole-in-one at the Danny Thomas Memphis Classic. It was the par three, 157-yard, fifth hole. I hit a five-iron shot that bounced once and rolled in. Incidentally, a generous family (with charitable judgment about my golfing accomplishment) paid $15,000 to St. Jude's Children's Hospital for that golf ball.

Oh, that golf was all unmitigated bliss. My friend Bob Hope has made a second career by capitalizing on my golf game. He calls me the "hit man for the P.G.A." He says his favorite foursome includes Jerry Ford, a faith healer, and a paramedic. He says that I have made golf a contact sport, and that I am the only guy who can play four courses—at the same time. He says he knew I was going to have a bad day when I lost two balls—in the ballwasher. He usually concludes this diatribe by saying, "The president played better the other day. He had an eagle, a birdie, an elk, a moose, and a Mason."

Bob says this all in jest, of course. His own golf tournament, in which I play, raises over $1 million each year for charity. I have a lot of fun with my own Jerry Ford Invitational Tournament in Vail, Colorado—an event that has raised about $750,000 for charities in that small community.

Actually, though, golf took up relatively little of my time in the months after I left the White House. I knew when I left office that the American people expected a former president to be constructive after his years in the White House. I tried to do that by spending nine weeks a year on college campuses; working two or three hours a day, seven days a week on my autobiography; contributing to television documentaries on serious subjects; and playing a role in the partisan political arena to insure that we have a strong, viable two-party system. During those first six months, when I logged more than 100,000 miles visiting thirteen states, I remember saying to Betty that it might be better to go back to the White House in 1980 to get some rest!

One thing I consciously decided not to do right after I left office was to criticize the new president. As Harry Truman once said, "Most presidents have received more advice than they can possibly use." A president has enough troubles without a former president beating him over the head every day. So I bit my tongue, at least for several months, even when I disagreed with some of President Carter's domestic policies.

I also tried to be helpful to my successor, especially in foreign policy. Over the course of his presidency, I can recall four instances when Jimmy Carter asked for my help in foreign policy: in the Senate to secure ratification of the Panama Canal Treaty; on the matter of recognizing the People's Republic of China; on the sale of aircraft to Egypt, Saudia Arabia, and Israel; and to help lift the arms embargo on Turkey. Those were areas where I could and did help my successor, and I was pleased to do so.

During my initial time out of office, I discovered a couple of things that continue to shape my public role as a former president. The first is that Americans have not decided what to do with their former presidents. Nothing in the Constitution addresses the issue; there are no laws prescribing a set role for former presidents—there is just very little in the way of guidance.

History offers little in the way of tradition. I have known seven former presidents personally. If you look at their activities after leaving office, you will be hard put to find a common pattern. What we do as former presidents is very much a matter of personal choice. To be sure, there are occasional obligations or expectations. But, in the main, what I have done since leaving the White House has been by my own choice and that is the way it ought to be. Frankly, I do not see the value in formalizing the role of former presidents. Historical circumstance, personal experience, and aptitude conspire against predetermined roles. Let former presidents decide what interest to pursue, what contributions to make, on their own.

My second observation is that media and technology, and the nature of public issues, afford the modern former president unprecedented opportunities to be innovative in his role and to remain in the public eye. The relative ease of travel, the ability of people to communicate quickly, and the almost instantaneous exposure of issues make conferences and symposia, for example, excellent forums for former presidents. Former presidents before me did not have these manifold chances to contribute to the timely discussion and resolution of policy issues.

Without prescribed activities and faced with a marvelous array of choices, I would venture to say that five themes have characterized my public life since leaving the White House. They relate to education, advocacy, partisanship, the celebrity status accorded a former president, and former presidents as symbols. Let me give you some examples.

The education role for former presidents comes in many shapes and sizes. I like to talk with students. At last count, I had visited over 170 colleges and universities and appeared before 600 classes, answering questions from students and faculty. I enjoy that because it gives me the chance to promote the feeling that each one of us can and does make a difference. I believe that we do, and I have seen it happen. I try to encourage young people to be optimistic, to take on responsibility, and to pursue their interests with vigor. You cannot always be the best, but you can always try your best.

My education work extends to many organizations. Through my association with the American Enterprise Institute, for example, I have hosted an annual World Forum in Vail, Colorado, involving economists, political figures, and business and government leaders from throughout the world. We have talked about such topics as the international debt crisis, exchange rates, arms control, and relations with the Soviets. My good friend, Helmut Schmidt, former chancellor of West Germany, said of these meetings: "What we have here is a beautiful experience: A conspiracy of former world leaders against present world leaders. But thank God none of us has the power to do anything anymore."

The work of the Gerald R. Ford Foundation and the Gerald R. Ford Library and Museum, for example, also serves the cause of education. Their conferences, exhibits, research, publications, and citizenship programs reach tens of thousands of people each year. If my status as a former president facilitates that kind of work—and I believe that it does—then I welcome it.

During the past twelve years, I have chosen to be an advocate as well as an educator. There are some substantial, consequential issues that concern me, and I have a long history with each of them. In fact, these issues represent continuity in my public life.

First, I am a proponent of limited government. A government that is big enough to give you everything you want is a government big enough to take everything you have. That is a message that bears repeating, and I believe it as an article of faith.

Second, I worry about the balance among the three branches of government. Although I spent twenty-five years in Congress, my time as president alerted me to the dangers of a weakened chief executive, especially in the conduct of foreign affairs. Our problem is not so much an "imperial" presidency as it is an "imperiled" presidency.

The War Powers Act, for example, limits presidential action in potentially dangerous terms. Passed in response to the Vietnam War, the resolution grants to Congress powers that, in my judgment, encroach on the constitutional prerogatives of the president as commander-in-chief. In April 1976, during the Easter holiday, I had to order U.S. forces to aid in the evacuation of our armed forces and Vietnamese allies from DaNang. During this congressional recess, I could not reach the members of the House and Senate with whom I was required to consult. There is absolutely no way American foreign policy can be conducted or military operations commanded by 535 members of Congress even if they all happen to be on Capitol Hill when they are needed.

A third issue on which I have taken a strong position is the congressional budget process. It continues to be a dismal failure. The Budget Reform and Anti-Impoundment Act has been in operation for fifteen years, but it has failed to bring coherence to the process and has, instead, saddled us with a bone-crushing debt. I have recommended specific changes to improve the budget process, and I have talked at length with key members of Congress and with my successor presidents about this very grave matter. In the meantime, the White House and the Congress ineffectively struggle annually with a federal budget that is out of control. The continuing high federal deficit is an economic time bomb. If my status as a former president helps us find a solution to these issues, then I welcome it.

Another role I have pursued involves partisan politics. Many people, especially those in the other party, told me that former presidents should be seen and not heard. But the quiet role of elder statesman held little appeal for me. I left office, but I did not leave politics. So I have traveled the country on behalf of the Republican party, promoting the candidacies of others, and helping to raise money for the party. I have spoken out repeatedly in favor of broadening the party's appeal and have resisted efforts to restrict it. Two vibrant, vital, political parties are at the core of our successful system of governing. Democracy is not a spectator sport. If my status as a former president promotes a competitive two-party system from top to bottom, then I welcome it.

Former presidents assume a celebrity status too—nothing to rival Bob Hope, of course—but there is a measure of celebrity status. I try to put that to good use on behalf of the Boy Scouts, for example. I am an old Eagle Scout, and I usually make six or eight speeches a year to benefit scouting and other worthy charitable causes. The philanthropic aspect of celebrity status is something that I share with Betty. She and I have raised funds for the Betty Ford Center, which treats individuals who have alcohol or other chemical dependencies. Betty is the real star of that effort as the "hands on" chairman of the board and frequent lecturer to the clinic's patients. Sometimes I feel as if I have seen all the thousand points of light that President Bush refers to, but if my status as a former president advances worthwhile charitable causes, then I welcome it.

Before I conclude, I would like to recall a highlight of my post-presidential career, one that illustrates the last of the themes—the symbolic importance of former presidents. In October 1981, three former presidents—Nixon, Carter, and I—met at the White House with then-President Ronald Reagan and, as it turned out, future President George Bush. This unprecedented and historic event came as the United States prepared to send its delegation to the funeral of Egyptian President Anwar Sadat. This event was the single most visible use of former presidents in my memory.

On the trip to Egypt, the former presidents (President Reagan and Vice President Bush did not accompany us) talked about what former presidents do—writing memoirs, building libraries, earning our living outside the White House. These are the threads that bind us together. We are an unusual fraternity, after all.

Moreover, I mark the beginning of my close association with Jimmy Carter with that trip. We joined together for an unprecedented interview on the way home, and since that time we have cooperated on a number of projects ranging from conferences to monitoring elections in Panama, to proposing an issues agenda for in-coming President George Bush.

We began as political adversaries, but now President Carter and I enjoy an easy rapport. When we travel together, we never have to search for things to talk about. We talk about our kids and grandchildren. We talk about our presidencies. We talk about what is going on in Washington. At no other time in our history, certainly not in this century, have two former presidents who were once opponents combined forces to advance the dialogue on the issues that face us all.

In this relationship with President Carter, I have learned that former presidents are accorded certain privileges. You are allowed to remember what you choose to remember and forget what you choose to forget. I do not remember ever saying anything bad about Jimmy Carter, and I do not remember Jimmy Carter ever saying anything bad about me. Ours is a fruitful relationship that we have put to good use.

I expect the future to be filled with the same opportunities and sense of accomplishment that I have enjoyed since leaving the White House. Betty and I have full schedules and we count ourselves fortunate if we can contribute in some small way to improving the quality of life in this nation that we so clearly love.

Former Presidents in American Public Life: A Guide to Further Reading and Research

TIMOTHY WALCH

The role of former presidents in American public life has not been of much interest to either scholars or political commentators until very recently. Once a president left office, the professors and the pundits turned their attention to his successor. The former president and his administration were confined to a few lines in the history books.

This did not mean that the American public had lost interest in their former leaders—far from it. In fact, many ex-presidents throughout American history have complained, both in public and in private, that they could not rid themselves of the celebrity of the office. The public often pestered these men to the point of distraction.

The recent emergence of former presidents as public political figures as well as celebrities has sparked interest in these men on the part of both historians and journalists. The scholars, for the most part, have focused on twentieth-century presidents from Theodore Roosevelt to Lyndon B. Johnson, writing brief essays or chapters on post-presidential activities. The journalists have concentrated on living former presidents from Richard M. Nixon to Ronald Reagan, publishing commentary on the specific activities of each man.

For all these books and articles, however, the topic has not been seriously or systematically studied. In this regard a useful primer is an article by Alan Evan Schenker, "Former Presidents: Suggestions for the Study of an Often Neglected

Resource," *Presidential Studies Quarterly* 12 (Fall 1982):545–551.

Historians have not made a great effort to survey the role of former presidents. The first survey appeared in 1925 with Winthrop Dudley Sheldon's *The Ex-Presidents of the United States: How Each Played a Role* (Philadelphia, 1925), but it would be fifty years before another historian approached the topic. Marie B. Hecht, *Beyond the Presidency: The Residue of Power* (New York, 1976), provides a topical analysis of the opinions and activities of former presidents, discussing war and peace, politics, making a living, literary lives, and other topics. It remains the best effort to date. Two other surveys that appeared in the 1980s are James C. Clark's *Faded Glory: Presidents Out of Power* (New York, 1985) and the most recent, Homer Cunningham, *The Presidents' Last Years: George Washington to Lyndon Johnson* (Jefferson, N.C., 1989). Neither of these surveys does much more than skim the surface of the topic.

Two studies of note that will lead scholars in the right direction are Donald R. McCoy's chapter on the presidential library system in his *The National Archives: America's Ministry of Documents, 1934–1968* (Chapel Hill, 1978) and Frank L. Schick et al., *Records of the Presidency: Presidential Papers and Libraries from Washington to Reagan* (Phoenix, 1989). Also of value is Fritz Viet, *Presidential Libraries and Collections* (Westport, Conn., 1987). Although these studies do not focus on the post-presidency, they do point to the best sources, namely the Manuscript Division of the Library of Congress and the presidential libraries.

Journalists and other commentators have examined former presidents in recent years. As their number has increased, from one in the 1940s to four in the 1990s, they have become more interesting. On occasion these writers ask what the proper role is for these men. For this literature, see

Robert L. Hardesty, "Squandered National Resource," *Newsweek* (March 14, 1977), "The Flight of Three Presidents," *Time* Magazine (October 26, 1981), "Catching Up on the Middle East," *Time* Magazine (November 21, 1983), George Hackett et al., "How to be an Ex-President," *Newsweek* (May 22, 1989), and Bernard Weisberger "Expensive Ex-presidents," *American Heritage* (May/June 1989).

The place to begin any research on the presidents of our era, the twentieth century, is *The Letters of Theodore Roosevelt*, edited by Elting E. Morison, 8 vols. (Cambridge, 1951–1954). Volumes seven and eight cover the post-presidential years, 1909 to 1919. Also of value are Roosevelt's writings published in a memorial edition shortly after his death. See *The Works of Theodore Roosevelt*, 24 vols. (New York, 1923–1926).

Scholars of the Roosevelt post-presidency will want to consult the extraordinary papers left by Roosevelt to the Library of Congress. The Library has microfilmed these papers and they are easily available through interlibrary loan. See *Index to the Theodore Roosevelt Papers*, 3 vols. (Washington, D.C., 1969).

Historians have devoted attention to Roosevelt's post-presidential period beginning with a popular account by Earle Looker entitled *Colonel Roosevelt: Private Citizen* (New York, 1932). George Mowry's *Theodore Roosevelt and the Progressive Movement* (Madison, 1946) remains a useful volume. William Manner discusses Roosevelt's breach and reconciliation with his successor, William Howard Taft, in *TR & Will* (New York, 1969). Joseph L. Gardner focuses directly on Roosevelt's post-presidential period in *Departing Glory: Theodore Roosevelt as Ex-President* (New York, 1973). A work that builds upon Mowry's account is *The Bull Moose Years: Theodore Roosevelt and the Progressive Party* by John Gable (Port Washington, N.Y., 1979).

The best available study of TR in his post-presidential years is John Milton Cooper's, *The Warrior and the Priest: Theodore Roosevelt and Woodrow Wilson* (Cambridge, 1983), especially pages 225–345. TR's high visibility during the last decade of his life appears in Lewis L. Gould's "The Price of Fame: Theodore Roosevelt as a Celebrity," *Lamar Journal of the Humanities* 10 (Fall 1984):7–18.

Like Roosevelt, William Howard Taft followed the tradition of leaving his papers to the Library of Congress. Also like Roosevelt, Taft had an active post-presidential career, first as dean of Yale University Law School, later as chief justice of the U.S. Supreme Court. The Library contains a substantial volume of manuscript materials on Mr. Taft's post-presidential career. See *Index to the William Howard Taft Papers* (Washington, D.C., 1972).

Unlike Taft himself, who weighed over 300 pounds, scholarship on the twenty-seventh president is slim. Henry Pringle's *The Life and Times of William Howard Taft*, 2 vols. (New York, 1939), is still the most complete biography. Taft's post-presidential years are covered in pages 856–1079 of Volume 2. A popular treatment is Ishbel Ross, *An American Family: The Tafts, 1678 to 1964* (Cleveland, 1964). Two studies have focused on Taft's legal career: Frederick C. Hicks, *William Howard Taft: Yale Professor of Law and New Haven Citizen* (New Haven, 1945) and Alpheus T. Mason, *William Howard Taft: Chief Justice* (New York, 1965).

After his presidency, Woodrow Wilson led a quiet, secluded ex-presidency in his S Street home in Washington. His body and mind ravaged by a stroke suffered in 1919, he was physically unable to do much after he left the White House. After her husband's death, Edith Wilson made an extensive effort to collect all of her husband's extant papers from friends and associates. The papers were used extensively by Mr. Wilson's authorized biographer, Ray Stannard Baker.

The papers eventually were donated by Mrs. Wilson to the Library of Congress and are available on microfilm. See *Index to the Woodrow Wilson Papers*, 3 vols. (Washington, D.C., 1973).

Given Wilson's stroke and seclusion in retirement, it is not surprising that historians have given short shrift to his ex-presidency. Typical is Arthur Walworth's *Woodrow Wilson: American Prophet and World Prophet*, 2 vols. (London, 1958), which devotes only 12 of 875 pages to Wilson's life after the White House. The one exception is a delightful book by Gene Smith entitled *When the Cheering Stopped: The Last Years of Woodrow Wilson* (New York, 1964).

Also of some value are two memoirs and two popular biographies of Edith Bolling Wilson. Mrs. Wilson's *My Memoir* (New York, 1939) is a very personal but not very accurate account of her husband's last years. Ishbel Ross's *Power with Grace: The Life Story of Mrs. Woodrow Wilson* (New York, 1975) includes a sympathetic and readable account of the Wilsons' life on S Street. Also of note is Tom Schachtman's *Edith and Woodrow: A Presidential Romance* (New York, 1981). In *Woodrow Wilson: An Intimate Memoir* (New York, 1960), Cary T. Grayson, Wilson's White House physician, provides a discreet discussion of Wilson's health after he left the White House.

Calvin Coolidge was as quiet in his post-presidential years as he was during his time in the White House. Unlike his predecessors and successors, Coolidge did not accumulate any body of post-presidential papers. The Coolidge Papers at the Library of Congress have no items that document the Coolidge presidency. The Library does have, however, the papers of Coolidge's secretaries, Edward Tracy Clark and Everett Sanders, which include some post-presidential letters from Coolidge. The Forbes Library in Northampton, Massachusetts, has a body of Coolidge Papers that the former president took with him when he left the White House. For a calendar, see Lawrence E. Wikander, ed., *A Guide to the Personal Files of President Calvin Coolidge* (Northampton, Mass., 1986). It notes a few post-presidential items.

Given the lack of source material, it is not surprising that Coolidge's post-presidential years have received very little attention from historians. Of note are Donald R. McCoy's *Calvin Coolidge: The Quiet President* (1967, Lawrence, Kansas. 1988), has a twenty-page account of Coolidge's retirement. See also Richard Norton Smith's "Calvin Coolidge: The Twilight Years," in *The Real Calvin Coolidge* (Plymouth, Vermont. 1986), and Alan Evan Schenker's, "Calvin Coolidge in Retirement: Public Life of a Private Citizen," *Presidential Studies Quarterly* 18 (Spring, 1988):413–426.

Lack of material is not a problem for biographers of Herbert Hoover. Indeed, the Hoover Presidential Library in West Branch, Iowa, contains hundreds of thousands of items documenting the most impressive post-presidential career in American history. During thirty-one years of activity after he left the White House, Hoover took on dozens of projects. There are 520 linear feet of archival boxes filled with documentation on the rich diversity of Hoover's interests and activities from the time he left the White House in 1933 until his death in 1964. See *Historical Materials in the Herbert Hoover Presidential Library* (West Branch, 1990).

Both the quality and the quantity of scholarship on Hoover's post-presidency is quite high. Of note are Gary Dean Best's encyclopedic *Herbert Hoover: The Post-Presidential Years, 1933–1964*, 2 vols. (Stanford, 1983) and Richard Norton Smith's *An Uncommon Man: The Triumph of Herbert Hoover* (1984, Worland, Wyoming. 1990). These are complementary works that document Hoover's determination to remain active in public life after his electoral defeat in 1932.

Hoover was a prolific author in the decades after his presidency and some of his books have remained in print more than twenty-five years after his death. Of note are *The Challenge to Liberty* (1934), a short critique of the New Deal; *On Growing Up* (1962), a wonderful collection of his correspondence with children; and *Fishing for Fun* (1963), a light-hearted compilation of Hoover's thoughts on one of his life-long passions. These three books have been reprinted by the Hoover Presidential Library Association and are available in paperback.

An important but often overlooked account by Hoover is *An American Epic*, 4 vols. (Chicago, 1959–1964), which details Hoover's extraordinary work in relieving famine and hunger throughout the world. The fourth volume chronicles Hoover's contributions after the presidency. Also of use is the eight-volume compilation of the former president's speeches after leaving the White House: *Addresses on the American Road* (New York and elsewhere, 1938–1961).

Of value are three general biographies of Hoover. A brief account of Hoover's post-presidency can be found in David Burner's *Herbert Hoover: A Public Life* (New York, 1979). Another brief but more substantive chapter is in Joan Hoff Wilson's *Herbert Hoover: Forgotten Progressive* (Boston, 1975). In *Herbert Hoover* (Boston, 1980), Wilton Eckley concentrates on the former president's writings, analyzing each book in detail.

Harry S. Truman was one president who thoroughly enjoyed his post-presidency, a fact that is reflected in the documentation and scholarly literature of this period of his life. His enthusiasm for life and the diversity of his post-presidential activities are documented in the 364 linear feet of papers that cover that period of his life, carefully preserved in the Harry S. Truman Library in Independence, Missouri. The papers include Truman's correspondence with other presidents and former presidents, notably his good friend Herbert Hoover, as well as with friends, politicians, and the public. See *Historical Materials in the Harry S. Truman Library* (Independence, 1987).

Historical writing on Truman's post-presidential years has been limited, however. The former president's daughter, Margaret Truman, published *Harry S. Truman* (New York, 1973), which has a brief account of her father's post-presidency. Charles Robbins's *Last of His Kind: An Informal Portrait of Harry S. Truman* (New York, 1979) is an illustrated biography that concentrates on the post-presidential years. Robert H. Ferrell's *Truman: A Centenary Remembrance* is another illustrated account that includes a section on the post-presidential years. See also Roy Jenkins's *Truman* (New York, 1986).

Several short essays are worthy of mention, such as Richard Rhodes, "Harry's Last Hurrah," *Harper's* Magazine 240 (January 1970):48–58, and James Giglio, "Harry S. Truman and the Multifarious Ex-Presidency," *Presidential Studies Quarterly* 12 (1982):239–255.

Certainly the most substantive body of work on the Truman post-presidency has come from the pen of Truman himself. In two books published during his lifetime and in another that appeared after his death, Truman provided his post-presidential views on a variety of subjects including "What to Do with Former Presidents," chapter in *Mr. Citizen* (New York, 1960). Also published in that year was *Truman Speaks* (New York, 1960), lectures that he gave at Columbia University in 1959. A less formal, even intimate Truman comes forth in Robert H. Ferrell's edited collection *Dear Bess: The Letters From Harry to Bess Truman, 1910--959* (New York, 1983).

Dwight D. Eisenhower did not have much in common with his predecessor except that both men had active post-presidential careers reflected in the holdings of their respective presidential libraries. Indeed, Eisenhower was very active as a former president, judging by the volume of papers in the Dwight D. Eisenhower Library in Abilene, Kansas. His post-presidential papers comprise approximately 1,000 cubic feet and cover the years from 1961 until his death in 1969.

The contents are as rich as they are voluminous and document Eisenhower's participation in Republican politics, his role as an informal foreign policy adviser to Presidents John F. Kennedy and Lyndon B. Johnson, his involvement in educational and other philanthropic causes, his writings for publication, his private business affairs, and his personal life. Of special interest will be the "Principal File," which consists of high-level materials arranged into subject and correspondence series. Many of these files are as yet closed, pending processing. See *Historical Materials in the Dwight D. Eisenhower Library* (Abilene, 1988).

Eisenhower's post-presidential activities have been included in a number of biographies, the best of which is Stephen E. Ambrose, *Eisenhower: The President* (New York, 1984). Also of significant value is Steve Neal, *The Eisenhowers: Reluctant Dynasty* (1978, Lawrence, Kansas. 1984), which discusses Ike's special relations with his brother Milton and his son, John. John S.D. Eisenhower adds much to the understanding of his father's post-presidency in *Strictly Personal* (New York, 1974). Also of value are Robert H. Ferrell's edition of *The Eisenhower Diaries* (New York, 1981), which includes a section on Ike's retirement, and Peter Lyons, *Eisenhower: Portrait of a Hero* (Boston, 1974), which briefly chronicles the post-presidential years.

Lyndon B. Johnson's post-presidential years await scholarly research. To be sure, aides and friends have commented on working with the former president, and a few have written about it. See the epilogue in Doris Kearns, *Lyndon Johnson and the American Dream* (New York, 1976); Mary Hardesty, "LBJ's Rambunctious Retirement," *Harper's Weekly* (January 24, 1975); and Harry J. Middleton, *LBJ: The White House Years* (New York, 1990)

There are also a few contemporary essays that will be of interest to students of the Johnson post-presidency. Of note are "After LBJ 'Retires' to Texas," *U.S. News and World Report* (December 23, 1968); "LBJ in Retirement—Still a Busy Man," *U.S. News and World Report* (September 29, 1969); "LBJ in Retirement: A Close-Up of an Ex-President," *U.S. News and World Report* (April 12, 1971).

More importantly, there is a substantial body of Johnson post-presidential materials in the Johnson Library on the campus of the University of Texas at Austin—nearly 500 linear feet of files that cover the years from 1969 until the president's death in 1973. For the most part these files are closed pending processing. Exceptions are the files on the CBS television interviews done in 1969–1970 and some files in the Name File series. See *Historical Materials in the Lyndon Baines Johnson Library* (Austin, 1988).

The living former presidents—Richard M. Nixon, Gerald R. Ford, Jimmy Carter, and Ronald Reagan—also present challenges to researchers on the role of former presidents. For the most part, the information on each must be gleaned from newspapers and magazines. All four remain active in public life and will, no doubt, continue to fascinate scholars and the general public.

The best source of information on Richard M. Nixon is the former president himself. Since 1980 he has written five books that give a clear presentation of his views on world affairs: *Real War* (New York, 1980); *Leaders* (New York, 1982); *Real Peace* (Boston, 1984); *No More Vietnams* (New York, 1986); and *1999: Victory Without War* (New York,

1988). His most recent book is *In the Arena: A Memoir of Victory, Defeat, and Renewal* (New York, 1990).

Mr. Nixon is active in the establishment of his presidential library in Yorba Linda, California, where he was born in 1913. Unlike other presidential libraries, however, the Nixon Library will not be administered by the National Archives and Records Administration. The Nixon Library doubtless will eventually receive and make available files related to Mr. Nixon's post-presidential career.

There is no end to the number of journalists who have commented on Mr. Nixon in retirement. The most complete study to date is Robert Sam Anson, *Exile: The Unquiet Oblivion of Richard Nixon* (New York, 1985). See also Anthony Lewis, "Still Nixon," *New York Times* (August 2, 1984); John Herbers, "After Decade, Nixon is Gaining Favor," *New York Times* (August 5, 1984); and Richard Bernstein, "Nixon's Reemergence: Limits and Possibilities," *New York Times* (April 15, 1988).

Like his predecessors and successor, Gerald R. Ford has remained active in public affairs after leaving the nation's highest office. And like fellow former presidents, Mr. Ford has established a presidential library that holds documentation on his post-presidency as well as his presidency. The Gerald R. Ford Library on the Ann Arbor campus of the University of Michigan contains more than 300 linear feet of post-presidential files covering the years from 1977 to 1988. For the most part these materials remain closed pending processing. Scrapbooks for the years from 1929 through the present are open and many have been microfilmed and are available via interlibrary loan. See *Historical Materials in the Gerald R. Ford Library* (Ann Arbor, 1987).

President Ford has yet to find a biographer, and researchers will find little in print concerning his retirement. In addition to many essays and the memoirs of his presidency,

Mr. Ford has published *Humor and the Presidency* (New York, 1987), a light-hearted look at how humorists—particularly cartoonists—have commented on American presidents. Robert M. Warner's "The Prologue is Past," *The American Archivist* 41 (1978):5–15 relates the establishment of the Ford Library at the University of Michigan. Also of value are two short essays by James Reston: "The Happiest Politician," *New York Times* (March 3, 1982), and "Jerry Ford at 70," *New York Times* (August 14, 1983). Robert Lindsey, "Busy Gerald Ford Adds Acting to Repertory," *New York Times* (December 19, 1983), provides information on some of Mr. Ford's post-presidential activities.

Jimmy Carter has been among the most active of former presidents and many of his interests are discussed in the memoir by Steven H. Hochman in this volume. Mr. Carter's base of operations is the Carter Presidential Center located in Atlanta, Georgia, which includes the Carter Center of Emory University and the Jimmy Carter Library and Museum. Records from the Carter Center will form the nucleus of Mr. Carter's post-presidential papers and eventually will be deposited in the Carter Library.

As with President Ford, no historian has as yet taken up Mr. Carter's post-presidency. Two recent journalistic assessments are Art Harris, "Citizen Carter: The Moral Imperative of the Former President and Peacemaker," *Washington Post* (February 22, 1990), and Wayne King, "Carter Redux," *New York Times Magazine* (December 10, 1989). Of similar interest are Mike Rosenberg, "Carter for Congress," *New York Times* (March 13, 1981); "Carter Joins Volunteers to Build Homes for the Poor" *Jet* (July 28, 1986); William E. Schmidt, "Reshaped Carter Image Tied to Library Opening," *New York Times* (September 21, 1986); Carol Lawson, "The Carters Make the Most of a New Life," *New York Times* (May 18, 1987); R. W. Apple, "Carter the Peacemaker Now Turns to

Ethiopia," *New York Times* (September 3, 1989); "Hail to the Ex-Chief," *Time* Magazine (September 11, 1989); and Jerry Schwartz, "Ethiopian Parlay Satisfying Carter," *New York Times* (September 21, 1989).

In addition to activities at the Carter Center, the former president has written several books since leaving office. In addition to the memoirs of his presidency, Mr. Carter has written *Negotiation: The Alternative to Hostility* (Macon, Ga. 1984), the Carl Vinson Memorial Lecture; *The Blood of Abraham* (New York, 1985), a discussion of the Middle Eastern turmoil; *Everything to Gain: Making the Most of the Rest of Your Life* (New York, 1987), written with Rosalynn Carter; and *An Outdoor Journal: Adventures and Reflections* (New York, 1988), which contains Mr. Carter's thoughts on and memories of fishing and other outdoor activities.

It is too soon to assess Ronald Reagan's post-presidential career. Like his predecessors during their first year out of office, Mr. Reagan is busy writing his memoirs and raising funds to establish his presidential library to be located in Thousand Oaks, California. One early speculation on Mr. Reagan's post-presidential activities is Andrew Rosenthal's, "Citizen Reagan Won't be a Retiree," *New York Times* (January 2, 1989).

Whatever Mr. Reagan decides to do in retirement, there will be no lack of input from the U.S. Congress. Defining a formal role for former presidents in American public life seems to be an irresistible urge on the part of Capitol Hill. Specific proposals to designate former presidents as honorary members of either the House or the Senate go back at least to 1916 when J. Hampton Moore of Pennsylvania introduced a bill to create permanent House seats for former presidents. See U.S. House of Representatives, *Congressional Record*, 64 Cong., 2nd Sess. (Washington, D.C., 1917):361.

Beginning in 1944 and for the next nineteen years in

sucession, members of both the House and the Senate introduced similar legislation to no avail. See U.S. Senate, *Congressional Record*, 88 Cong., 1st Sess. (Washington, D.C.,
1963):1393–1394, 18516–18517, for a typical resolution
introduced in 1963 by Claiborne Pell of Rhode Island. The
most recent effort to make former presidents members of
the House was introduced on May 10, 1989, by Wayne
Owens of Utah, but no action has been taken on this bill.
See U.S. House of Representatives, *Congressional Record*, 101
Cong, 1st Sess. (Washington D.C., 1989):E1615.

Contributors

STEPHEN E. AMBROSE is Alumni Distinguished Professor of History at the University of New Orleans. He is the author of many books including a widely heralded two-volume biography of Dwight D. Eisenhower. The second volume of his three-volume biography of Richard Nixon was published in September 1989.

DANIEL J. BOORSTIN is Librarian of Congress Emeritus. The recipient of the Pulitzer, Bancroft, and Parkman prizes among others, Dr. Boorstin is widely known for his three-volume history, *The Americans*, and for *The Discoverers*, a history of man's search for the world and himself.

JOHN V. BRENNAN is a former chief of staff to President Richard M. Nixon. He currently is the president of Brennan International, a Washington-based consulting firm.

JOHN MILTON COOPER, JR., is chairman of the Department of History and William Allen Francis Professor of History at the University of Wisconsin. He is the author of many books including *The Warrior and the Priest*, a study of Theodore Roosevelt and Woodrow Wilson.

ROBERT H. FERRELL is Distinguished Professor of History Emeritus at Indiana University. A prolific and prize-winning author, Dr. Ferrell has written and edited many studies of the presidency including *Woodrow Wilson and World War I* and *Harry S. Truman and the Modern American Presidency*.

GERALD R. FORD was the thirty-eighth President of the United States. His memoirs of his presidential service are published in *A Time to Heal: The Autobiography of Gerald R. Ford*. President Ford continues to serve his nation as an adviser to succeeding presidents and to the heads of foreign governments who request his advice.

LEWIS L. GOULD is Eugene C. Barker Centennial Professor of History at the University of Texas. Dr. Gould is a member of the Board of Editors of *Presidential Studies Quarterly* and the author of a number of books on the presidency including studies of William McKinley, Theodore Roosevelt, and Woodrow Wilson.

ROBERT L. HARDESTY is the former president of Southwest Texas State University, the alma mater of President Lyndon B. Johnson. From 1965 to 1972 he served as an assistant to President Johnson and later served as the chairman of the Board of Governors of the U.S. Postal Service.

FRANCIS H. HELLER is Roy A. Roberts Distinguished Professor of Law and Political Science Emeritus at the University of Kansas. In 1954–1955, Professor Heller assisted President Harry S. Truman with his memoirs. He also has written twelve books including *The Presidency: A Modern Perspective* and *The Truman White House*.

STEVEN H. HOCHMAN is assistant to President Jimmy

Carter and senior research associate at the Carter Center of Emory University where he assists President Carter with his academic and scholarly affairs. From 1968 to 1981 Dr. Hochman assisted Dumas Malone with his prize-winning, six-volume biography of Thomas Jefferson.

DAVID McCULLOUGH is host of the popular public television series, "The American Experience." Mr. McCullough also is the author of several prize-winning books including *The Path Between the Seas*, about the Panama Canal, and *Mornings on Horseback*, a biography of the young Theodore Roosevelt. He is at work on a biography of Harry S. Truman.

DONALD R. McCOY is University Distinguished Professor of History at the University of Kansas. Dr. McCoy is a member of the Board of Editors of *Presidential Studies Quarterly* and the author of biographies of Alf Landon and Calvin Coolidge. Most recently he published *The Presidency of Harry S. Truman*.

HARRY J. MIDDLETON is director of the Lyndon Baines Johnson Library and formerly served as assistant to President Johnson in the preparation of his memoirs. Mr. Middleton recently completed a pictorial biography of President Johnson entitled *LBJ: The White House Years*.

ROGER MUDD is special correspondent for the "MacNeil/ Lehrer News Hour." He formerly served as senior political correspondent and news anchor for the "NBC Nightly News" and the "CBS Evening News."

GEORGE H. NASH is the author of a multivolume biography of Herbert Hoover, of which two volumes have appeared. Dr. Nash also is the author of a number of other works including *The Conservative Intellectual Movement in America Since 1945*.

STEVE NEAL is a columnist and political editor with the *Chicago Sun-Times* and the former White House correspondent for the *Chicago Tribune*. Mr. Neal is the author of five books on American politics including biographies of Wendell Willkie and the Eisenhowers.

RICHARD NORTON SMITH is director of the Herbert Hoover Library and Museum. Mr. Smith formerly served as a speechwriter for Senators Pete Wilson and Robert Dole, among others. He is the author of five books including *An Uncommon Man: The Triumph of Herbert Hoover*.

HELEN THOMAS is the White House bureau chief for United Press International and the dean of White House correspondents. Ms. Thomas has known and reported on every American president since John F. Kennedy. The recipient of ten honorary doctorates, she also is the author of *Dateline: White House*.

TIMOTHY WALCH is assistant director of the Herbert Hoover Library and Museum. The author or editor of ten books, Dr. Walch served as editor of *Prologue: Quarterly of the National Archives* from 1982 to 1988.

DON W. WILSON is Archivist of the United States and, as such, is responsible for directing the work of the National Archives and Records Administration. Dr. Wilson previously served as director of the Gerald R. Ford Library and Museum and as assistant director of the Dwight D. Eisenhower Library.

Index

Sadat, Anwar, 124, 127, 176
San Clemente, California, 119, 120
San Francisco, California, 86, 87
Saturday Evening Post, 10, 14, 18
Scranton, William, 72, 84, 86
Secret Service, 11, 20, 48, 67, 120, 121
Senate, vii, xi, 16, 62, 69, 85, 102, 141, 149, 172
Smith, Richard Norton, 25, 196
Southeast Asia, 74, 75, 76, 104
South Vietnam, 75, 85
Soviet Union, 26, 31, 71, 73
Speaker of the House, 139, 143
Speeches by former presidents, 13, 33, 35, 130, 152, 161
Stalin, Josef, 29, 31, 51
Stanford University, 32
State Department, 83, 84
Stevenson, Adlai E., 59, 60, 61, 82, 165

Taft, Robert, 40, 89
Taft, William Howard, vii, xi, xii, 1, 10, 11, 12, 14, 15, 16, 20, 133
Television appearances by former presidents, 56, 102-106, 140, 143, 159, 160, 162, 163, 171
Texas, 96, 97, 98, 102, 107
Third party candidates, 5, 6
Thomas, Helen, xiii, 152, 161, 164, 196
Time, 123, 125
Travel by former presidents, 33, 35, 98
Truman, Bess, 47, 48, 54, 55
Truman, Harry, viii, 30, 31, 32, 45, 47, 48, 52, 55, 56, 76, 82, 85, 88, 102, 104, 105, 127, 146, 147, 151, 153, 155, 171
Truman Library, xiv, 49, 57, 62
Twenty-second Amendment, 65, 68, 80, 90, 140

University of Michigan, 131, 163

Vail, Colorado, 161, 170, 173
Van Buren, Martin, vii, 5, 55, 140

Vermont, 17, 147
Vietnam, 62, 71, 73, 77, 78, 102, 174. *See also* Southeast Asia
Virginia, xii, 127, 133

Walch, Timothy, 179, 196
Waldorf Astoria Towers, 33, 34, 39
Washington, D.C., 10, 18, 25, 47, 55, 123, 146, 148
Washington, George, vii, ix, 127
West Branch, Iowa, 147, 152
Westmoreland, William, 74, 75
White House, 3, 11, 13, 30, 37, 55, 73, 77, 82, 96, 99, 119, 124, 125, 140, 151, 153, 164, 170, 175, 176
Wilson, Don W., xiii, 163, 196
Wilson, Woodrow, vii, 1, 3, 4, 5, 7, 8, 10, 12, 33
World War I, ix, 6, 12, 16, 29, 38, 42
World War II, 29, 38

Yale University, xii, 12, 14, 52
Yorba Linda, California, 121, 152